AFTER I'M GONE

HUMAN HORIZONS SERIES

AFTER I'M GONE

What Will Happen To My Handicapped Child?

GERALD SANCTUARY

*Legal Adviser to the Royal
Society for Mentally
Handicapped Children & Adults*

A CONDOR BOOK
SOUVENIR PRESS (E & A) LTD

ISBN 0 285 64991 4 casebound
ISBN 0 285 64992 2 paperbound

Photoset and printed in Great Britain by
Photobooks (Bristol) Ltd

Contents

Preface

During the five years I have worked with the Royal Society for Mentally Handicapped Children and Adults I have been asked, time and time again, what parents can do, during their lives and afterwards, by their wills, to ensure a secure and happy life for their children in the years to come.

Parents' feelings are deep, and often agonising. I have been greatly concerned while writing this book, lest some of the examples I give and suggestions I make may themselves cause distress. How could it be otherwise? The thought of leaving one's loved child is more than many parents can bear to contemplate. I can only say that my intention is not to hurt or to distress a single parent or relative, but only to make suggestions which I hope will result in a better future for their children. In particular, I hope that the plan I describe in Chapter 9 will be very carefully considered by parents. I believe that it may be capable of improving the prospects for many handicapped people.

This book has many references to people with mental handicap, and to Mencap (which is the short title of the Royal Society for Mentally Handicapped Children & Adults). As my work is with the Royal Society, I have naturally drawn on my own experience. There are in fact more people with mental handicap than all other forms of handicap added together, except of course old age. Fortunately, however, the majority of what is written here applies just as much to those who are physically handicapped as it does to those who suffer from mental handicap.

I have added Appendices I and II in the hope that they will be of help to my fellow solicitors. I have not been able to find, in one place, a reference to the various statutes, regulations and decided cases that especially affect handicapped people, and these I have included. I have also set down what I hope will be some useful draft clauses for wills and trusts.

I am grateful to those colleagues at the Royal Society who have helped me with the preparation of the book, particularly Mr R. Hermelin and Mrs M. Robottom, and, most of all, to the many parents of handicapped children who have helped me by describing the problems they face, and the questions they want answered.

Gerald Sanctuary
St. Albans
January 1984

1   A Growing Problem

Most handicapped children live at home with their parents. Only a minority are in hospitals, group homes or hostels run by Local Authorities, or homes and villages organised by charities. In the past, the great majority of handicapped people tended to die before their parents, but advances in medical science, and in treatment, have brought about a great change. Today, a very large number of handicapped children are outliving both their parents.

As a result, a great many parents are now asking: 'After I'm gone, what will happen to my handicapped child?'

There is no single answer that will apply to each and every family; their circumstances differ, as do the degrees of handicap of their children. The policies of Social Services Departments throughout the country are by no means identical. The same is true of hospitals and Health Authorities. Even the way in which the regulations for social security benefits are applied seem to differ from one area to another. The provision of homes, and of practical support by local and national charities, are not the same in all parts of the country, because they depend on people and on the resources available, and on the policies of the Local Authorities.

The condition of some people with a handicap can improve, while others may deteriorate. Some, with support and a good training programme, can become far more competent than they are now. Some families can continue to care for a handicapped brother and sister after the parents have died or have become too old to cope; others cannot. Often, the parents have some resources, such as a house, which they would like to see used for the benefit of their child, but they do not see how this can be arranged. Regulations laid down by Parliament can very easily frustrate their intentions.

As more handicapped children outlive their parents, so the problem grows. Professional people, such as lawyers and social workers, are often not aware of the ways in which the general law and the various statutory regulations operate, and are unable to help. Indeed, there are many cases where bad advice has been given, and others where the law has changed, making it necessary for people to alter their wills and the arrangements they have made. It is a jungle, with traps for the unwary, and with the paths hard to find. The aim of this book is to act as a guide, and to explain in personal, practical and legal terms, the problems that exist and the best ways to avoid or overcome them.

Mr and Mrs Adams have a son, William, who is now 40 years old. He never received any schooling, because he had grown up before the Education Act 1970 came into effect in 1971 and gave all handicapped people the right to an education. The diagnosis is that he is mentally handicapped, probably through brain damage at or around the time he was born. His mother is 72, and his father 76. William lives with them at home. He has a quiet and contented life, and goes each day to an Adult Training Centre, where he helps to make nest-boxes for birds, and other garden items. Although it was once suggested that he might make his own way to the Centre, using public transport, his mother was very much opposed to this, as she worried lest something might happen to William on the way. He might get lost, she thought, or mocked by young people travelling on the bus. As a result, William goes to and from the Centre by special transport provided by the Local Authority; he leaves home at 8.30 am, and is usually back before 5.15 pm. At the Centre he is paid £4.00 pocket money each week, and he spends this on sweets and gramophone records. He can also spend money at the local Gateway Club, which he attends on Wednesday evenings, where coffee, tea, Coca-Cola and biscuits are available.

William goes on outings with the Gateway Club. He used to play football there, but because he gets very little exercise and is allowed to eat whatever he wants, he has become overweight. His parents do not normally take him out walking, as this can sometimes be a little embarrassing for them, and since Mr Adams retired he has had to give up the car he used to drive. At home, William watches television a lot. He can keep himself clean, but his mother has always done all the cooking for him. She tidies his room and makes sure he is properly dressed. He could probably manage more for himself, but he happily accepts the fact that his mother does everything; in a way, he has been trained to expect that this will happen. Once a year, the three of them go to a boarding house by the sea, where the landlady and the other guests know William, and where Mr and Mrs Adams feel accepted. They used to go by car, but now they go by long-distance bus, which William very much enjoys.

Over the last ten years or so, Mr and Mrs Adams have become increasingly anxious. They are wondering what will happen to William when they die or have become too old to care for him. What used to be something of an anxiety for them has become an obsession, and at times it drives them close to despair. The only local provision for mentally handicapped people is a large Victorian hospital. The wards there each hold 24 people, and there are not enough staff to provide personal care; they do their best, but there is simply no time for them to sit and talk with the 'patients', as they are called. Some are of course more handicapped than others, and are receiving sedatives and other medicines. People like William do not require medical care, except during an occasional illness, but they are in a hospital because there is nowhere else for them to go.

The County Council Social Services Department does have a hostel, nearly 30 miles away, where some mentally handicapped people live. It used to have a few short-stay places, but after a while the pressure of numbers became too great, and all the residents are now living there permanently. There is a waiting list, and several people there now have to share a room. As in the hospital, the staff at the hostel do their best, but because there are so many handicapped people to be fed and cared for, the atmosphere is that of an institution. Recently, the mother of a local handicapped woman died, and the Local Council sent her to stay in a private boarding house in North Wales, over a hundred miles from her home town. The Local Authority pays the fees of the boarding house, but no one ever visits her there. Mr and Mrs Adams do not want William to go into hospital, nor to the hostel (even if a bed were available there, which at present it is not). Nor do they want him to be sent to a place far from his home, his friends, his Gateway Club, and the Training Centre.

Mr Adams has been making enquiries: it turns out that in the area of the County Social Services Department there are now 80 mentally handicapped people living at home with one or more parents who are themselves 75 years, or even older. These are the men and women of whom the County knows; there are probably many more, but no assessment has been made of them. The problem facing these parents is even more urgent than that which concerns Mr and Mrs Adams who are still both in reasonably good health. It cannot be long before all these 80 people will have to be cared for by someone else, yet there is no provision ready for them, or even planned. Cuts in Government expenditure and general spending restrictions make it very unlikely that new facilities will be created in sufficient numbers to meet the need. Yet whether anything is done or not, a massive social problem is gradually building up, because handicapped people are living much longer than in the past. William is only one of many thousands for whom no provision has been made, but who will soon be the responsibility of the Social Service or Health Authorities.

Mr and Mrs Adams do have another child, Jack, who lives not far away. He is married and has three children of his own. He has always been fond of William and might be willing to look after him when the time comes, but his wife rejects the idea. 'I married you, not your brother,' she once said. She does not dislike William, but she is certainly not going to have him, as she puts it, 'under her feet all day'. This is mainly because William can do so little for himself, having been given no training by his mother, or by anyone else. Jack's wife has a job now that her children are growing up and does not want to become, in her own words 'a permanent baby-sitter'. In any event, Mr and Mrs Adams have never felt it would be fair for Jack to have to shoulder the burden that they have been carrying for 40 years. Having a handicapped brother imposed its own restrictions on Jack's life, and they do not think he should be expected to do more than keep an eye on William's health and welfare, after they have died.

Mr Adams recently visited the mental handicap hospital to which, it seems, William may have to go. On his return he could not bring himself to tell his wife what the conditions there were like. He saw no signs at all of cruel treatment, but he could see that the patients were living a soulless existence. He saw more than thirty of them in a large room, sitting in broken-down armchairs, listlessly watching television, or rocking aimlessly backwards and forwards. The television was fixed high up on the wall to prevent it being damaged. He felt that anyone living in such conditions, handicapped or not, would soon become abnormal, simply because of the surroundings.

As parents get older, they find it more and more difficult to look after themselves and their handicapped child. On retirement, the family car may be given up and they may have to rely on public transport. Heavy work, especially lifting a son or daughter who is physically handicapped, becomes ever more difficult. Illnesses are more frequent, and as time goes on older people find themselves less able to manage the things that they used to. Visits to the shops are less frequent; climbing ladders and lifting boxes become more difficult. Sometimes, the parents' sight or hearing starts to deteriorate, and this makes it much harder for them to meet the needs of their handicapped child who by this time is of course an adult. While all this is happening, their income has probably dropped and they are having to live on a pension. Even the modest level of the Supplementary Benefit provided by the State for their handicapped child, with some additions, makes all the difference. The Benefit may only maintain a person at the minimum level, but it can balance the budget of a couple who are finding it hard to maintain their standard of living.

It is small wonder that Mr and Mrs Adams, and many other parents like them, are driven to despair. Their situation is typical, not exceptional, and it is in no way exaggerated. There are no villains who can be easily identified, and blamed. One could criticise Mrs Adams for doing so much for her son and thereby reducing the chance that he will be able to live in homely surroundings; but this would be hardly fair, as there was never anyone to advise her, nor to explain that she was holding him back and not really helping him. One could blame the Local Council for making so little provision and for failing to plan ahead, to the extent that handicapped people are either being sent a hundred miles away from home, or put in a hospital. People can, and do, attack the Government for failing to tackle the problem, which grows more desperate as each year passes. Yet the Government says that national resources are limited. Both national and local government are having to provide for an increasing number of old people, as well as those who are physically or mentally handicapped. The tendency now is to provide a service only when the need is both immediate and urgent.

Something must be done. Parents and families of handicapped people must be given the maximum of information on what is practicable. Pressures must be brought on the Authorities to make plans, and to take action before conditions worsen to the point where they have become a public scandal. Yet it is not enough to bring pressure on the Authorities; parents, working individually and together, can themselves improve the prospects for their children.

Something can be done. Through planning, through education and training of handicapped people, and through the wise use of the limited resources of families, it is possible to make matters easier rather than worse. Action must be taken early rather than late, and joint planning - with other parents - is much better than individual effort. Parents and families can help their own handicapped son or daughter, but it is important that they begin to do this before they become too old or tired to act effectively.

The years have crept up on Mr and Mrs Adams; if they had been able to plan ahead, they would have wanted to ensure that, in the future, William would have a comfortable home and be well cared for. Ideally, they would have wished to see him settled in such a place some time before they began to feel their age. They would have been able to visit him regularly and the strain on them both, especially Mrs Adams, would have been much less. In addition, it would have been best if William could have been helped, from the time he began to grow up, to begin to look after himself, so far as he possibly could. Probably, he could have been trained to keep his own room tidy, dress himself and even prepare simple meals. Many other people like him have been able to do this. While some parents cannot bring themselves to allow their handicapped children to take risks and to make mistakes in the process of learning, others have shown that it can be done. Unfortunately, many parents have not been aware that training of this kind was available, and have not been able to act early enough to help their handicapped child manage some things for himself. Mrs Adams, on being told that a training course existed in the neighbourhood which might be able to help her son, said:

'Oh yes, but William could never manage that.'

Mr and Mrs Adams have not made wills. They thought about it only when Mr Adams retired, and they were so bewildered that they never did anything about it. They could have made arrangements for their property, small though it is, to be used to help William and improve his situation, instead of leaving him totally reliant on what the State will provide. They could have taken steps to ensure that someone, as well as his brother Jack, would be available to look after his interests, visit him regularly to see if he was reasonably fit and happy, and act generally as both a friend and advocate. They could have taken advice on the best way to entrust Jack with some money or other property, to use for William's benefit. This is not as easy to achieve as some people think. They could have made sure that Jack understands the State Benefits system, and the way in which the law affects handicapped people. Sadly, they did none of these things, and the prospect for William is bleak.

The older people become, the less likely it is that they will be able to take action. Yet the less action they take, the more difficult it will be to provide for their child's future. The purpose of this book is to explain what can be done; its message is that plans for the future of a handicapped child should be made as early as possible, if they are to be effective. Too late can mean too little.

2 A Style of Life

Think of your own childhood, and the way you grew up. As the years went by you began to separate yourself from your parents and adopted a life-style of your own. You accepted much of what they said and did what they wanted – most of the time – but you had to make your own way. You left school, got a job, married, found a home of your home, and began to create a life that was different.

Does your handicapped child have any right to a life-style of his own? Is he entitled to go his own way, to rebel, to reject your advice, to make mistakes? For many parents, the answer to these questions will be: 'Well, he couldn't. He needs someone to look after him.'

So he does; but should those who care for him make every decision, do everything for him? Has he no right to make any decisions for himself? In recent years it has become ever more clear that those who suffer from handicap are 'people with a handicap', rather than 'handicapped people'. They have as much right to a life of their own as the rest of us. Decisions should not be made for them, unless there is no prospect at all of their having an opinion to express.

The title of the BBC Radio programme *Does He Take Sugar?* cleverly illustrates the assumption made by most people that, simply because someone has to use a wheelchair, or is blind, he is incapable of thinking or of expressing a preference. This attitude is nonsense, and it is of course bitterly resented by those who suffer from physical handicap. There is another common assumption: that because a person is mentally handicapped he is incapable of making any sensible decision at all. It is just as insulting to a mentally handicapped woman to assume that she has no views to express about her life, as it is to ask the man pushing a wheelchair whether its occupant takes sugar with his tea.

The point is that handicapped people are entitled to a life of their own, just like everyone else. They have preferences, and it is wrong of society to ignore these. The progress that a handicapped person makes in life, and his happiness, must depend on the chance he is given to live his own life and to make his own choices. Simply because he will sometimes make mistakes does not entitle the rest of us to remove all choice from him; we, too, have made mistakes, but we have survived and are the wiser for it.

This argument cannot be taken to ridiculous lengths: a blind person must be discouraged from walking near a cliff edge; a woman in a wheelchair will require help in getting up a ramp; a mentally handicapped man must be protected from entering into an expensive hire purchase contract which he cannot possibly afford. Yet this does not prevent the blind man from going out on his own, nor the woman in a wheelchair; nor should it stop a mentally handicapped person from entering into simple contracts, such as buying food or records, or travelling on a bus.

If we start with the assumption that there will be many things that a handicapped person can do and is entitled to do, and if we positively encourage him in this, we are helping to create the chance for him to develop his own style of life. His handicap must be assessed, and the right type of education, and also training, found for him. He should have the chance to enjoy leisure activities, and to choose those he likes best. Throughout this book ways are suggested by which this can be achieved. If a parent has become used to doing many things for a handicapped child, it is worth considering when it might be possible for him to do some of them for himself. His Supplementary Benefit is his own, not his parents'; he can be taught how to draw the money for himself, and asked to give enough to his mother for her to buy food. Perhaps he would like to make some of his own decisions on clothes and other things.

What does a handicapped person want? This is a better question than 'What do we think is good for him?' The answer is not simple. If he is not aware that he has a choice, or has never been asked to make one, then he may happily accept the benevolent decisions of his parents. Matters of this kind are not confined to food or a choice of television programmes. Arthur Melsby enjoyed his walks in the park with his parents. He usually travelled in a wheelchair, but he was able to get around slowly, using a stick. He was a not a communicative young man and was regarded at school (which he had recently left) as very shy, if not backward. His brothers and sisters were talkative, often noisy, and because he was both handicapped and quite small he seemed almost to shrink into the background, in any group of people.

In the Summer, a brass band played in the park. Arthur heard it once and was fascinated. They were playing at a time when he did not normally go to the park, but he demanded to go again, even offering to make his own way there, almost half-a-mile from home. It was not very convenient for his family, but arrangements were made to take him again. It was impossible to persuade him to leave until the band packed up. One of the players noticed him and stopped for a word, asking him whether he had enjoyed the performance. Arthur asked if he could hold the trumpet that the man was carrying. This was only the beginning of what was for Arthur an entirely new life: he said he wanted to learn to play a brass instrument. His family helped him and took him to and from a college of music. After a while, this took so much time that it was necessary to hire a taxi to take him there and back. His Mobility Allowance paid for part, though not all, of the cost, but one of the teachers at the college had a car and would often give him a lift home. Arthur began to play the french horn; within a year he had become reasonably good, and after three years he joined an orchestra.

His life was transformed; at home he had brass band music on the gramophone, and he practised constantly. His room had to be insulated for sound, as the rest of the family found the noise distracting, but he persevered.

Arthur had found the life he wanted, and he never looked back. His determination might have been frustrated by a family less willing to help him branch out on his own, and less able to put up with the noise. When his brothers and sisters complained, their parents reminded them of the noise they also made, and they accepted the situation. In fact, no one felt any more that they had to 'keep Arthur occupied' or to amuse him; he was more than capable of entertaining himself. His new-found confidence, based on having been selected for the orchestra, changed both his style of life and his spirit.

Arthur was physically but not mentally handicapped. Moira Thorogood suffered from Down's Syndrome; she was short and had become plump. In the town she was well known to many people, trailing along beside her mother or father on shopping day, cheerful enough, but giving more the impression of a young child than a woman. She was 32 years old and not in fact very severely handicapped. Through a social club to which her parents belonged, arrangements were one day made for Moira to help with the catering. Her mother cooked small cakes and biscuits once a month, taking her turn with other members. Moira went with her, and on that particular day was invited to put out the cups and saucers. Her mother was very concerned in case there should be an accident, but the lady who encouraged Moira was persistent, though very friendly; she had helped at a school for physically handicapped children and assumed that Moira would like to do something useful.

After a while, Moira became an essential member of the social club, doing valuable work in and out of the kitchen. She broke no more cups or saucers than anyone else and was delighted to be able to make herself useful. Her parents, after some initial embarrassment, became very proud of what Moira could do. Later, she was asked to help in a local restaurant. She enjoyed it very much and spent most of her time working in the kitchen. She was paid a full wage and no longer needed to draw Supplementary Benefit. Her take-home pay was more than the Benefit and she had some extra money to spend on herself. Like Arthur Melsby, Moira had found a life-style which suited her very well indeed.

Given different opportunities and less encouragement from the families and friends, Arthur and Moira might today be in totally different situations, he confined for the most part to his home, with few outside contacts and dependent on his family for entertainment, she going to and from a Training Centre with little prospect of meeting people and taking part in the life of the community. Neither of them, as it happens, had been given training before deciding to branch out into new activity, but both have in fact been trained - in their different ways - as a result of finding a new interest.

Most parents will want to know what their child can be expected to achieve, given the right training and, of course, the right family support. Training centres do exist, providing residential facilities, where handicapped people can learn skills in horticulture, agriculture and the building trades. Handicapped people are no less entitled to this form of training, which is a form of further education, than anyone else, and Local Education Authorities have powers to give grants to support them.

Many students leaving school will find the college of further education, polytechnic or university of their choice and will make their own application. Those who have a handicap may need help to achieve the equivalent form of training to suit them. This is where the parents and other relatives should expect to give help. They may obtain application forms, investigate the courses that are available and visit the offices of the Local Education Authority to see what form of support is likely to be given. It may be wise, in the first instance, to obtain a formal assessment, and this should be done before the handicapped person leaves school. This is a legal entitlement and is described later.

The aim of one further education establishment is to train its students, all of whom are handicapped, to attain the greatest degree of independence that they can achieve. Some, of course, cannot go very far along this road and will always need help and guidance. Yet even they will be helped to manage as much for themselves as they possibly can. At the end of their two-year course, many of them return home to parents who are astonished at the progress achieved in social competence. Some are able to take up work in the community, as there is a special arrangement with the Parks Department of the Local Authority. Others have been trained in building skills and have been active, under the guidance of a qualified instructor, in repairing and renovating an old school-house and a stable block not far from the main building where they live. The result is that about thirty more places have been made available for handicapped people who are themselves also now receiving training. Apart from skilled specialists, such as a plumber and an electrician, all the work of renovating the buildings has been done by the handicapped people themselves, directed only by the instructor. They are justifiably proud of what they have done and glad to show it to visitors and parents, many of whom find it difficult to believe that it is the work of people who were labelled as 'handicapped', and assumed to be incapable of doing work of any difficulty.

There is a moral to this story: it is wrong to assume that a person with a handicap – even with quite a severe disability – is unable to perform a useful role in society. The difficulty is for parents and relatives to find the right type of training course, and to ensure that the young handicapped person can get the necessary grant from the Education Authority. In Appendix IV there is a list of names and addresses of various organisations who may be able to help and advise.

To make our way in the world, we need more than training for a specific job: we also need social training, the chance to enjoy leisure, and the opportunity to work. We are emotional and physical beings, whether we are handicapped or not. The parent who thinks that, because a child is handicapped, he or she has no capacity for adult emotions, is making a mistake and may be building up great trouble for the future. For example, handicapped people – like anyone else – need appropriate sex education.

One problem is that a great many people equate sex education with sex instruction, meaning 'how to have sex'. Of course, this is wrong. Sex education and sex instruction are not the same. In fact, every one of us receives sex education of one kind or another, good or bad, whether we have been told 'the facts of life' or have had any kind of sexual experience. We see dramas and films on television in which men and women come close to one another. We are bombarded by advertisements which encourage us to look and smell more attractive, and which play on our fears of being rejected. In a much more healthy context, we see our family, our friends and acquaintances expressing fondness, affection and love for one another. There is of course nothing wrong with this: it is part of normal life. It is ridiculous to suppose that we can, or should, try to prevent handicapped children from noticing what everyone else notices. We want them to be as normal as possible, and this means that they must be allowed to develop relationships with one another.

This most certainly does not mean that a handicapped person should be encouraged into a situation where she or he is liable to be sexually manipulated or harmed in any way. Some handicapped people may be less able than others to control their sexuality, and they will need greater care in helping and teaching them about sex. A handicapped girl, for example, should be protected from being injured or frightened, and from the risks of an unwanted pregnancy. Simply because sex education is taking place – whether planned or not – does not mean that sexual intimacy is to be positively encouraged, regardless of the effect it will have. At the same time, the sexual taboos that have always existed concerning human sexuality have lingered longer in relation to handicapped people than they have for the rest of our society. There is an assumption made by many of us that, because a person is mentally or physically handicapped, he has no sexual feelings, and that any tendency to express physical tenderness or love should be actively discouraged. We do not ask such restraint of our normal children; how can we demand it of those who are handicapped? The answer to this question is that many of us do demand it, because the idea of sexuality and handicap is profoundly distressing to us. Instead, we would be wiser to look at the reality, and not to close our eyes. A person's handicap does not necessarily deprive him or her of all normal feelings. We shall do harm if we pretend that it does.

It is a matter of balance. On the one side, it is irresponsible to encourage a handicapped person into a situation which she cannot handle. On the other, it cannot be right to deprive her of a social life, and of close affection. In the end, the decision will be that of the parents, who should try to help their child live the life of a normal person who suffers from a handicap, not of an abnormal individual who cannot be allowed to make a loving relationship.

In the eyes of the law, as soon as a handicapped person reaches the age of 18 he may do what he wishes, just as any other person of the same age can do. Until the contrary is proved, he is assumed to be able to make his own decisions and determine the course of his own life. What, then, if he - or she - decides to get married? If the handicapped person suffers only from physical and not mental handicap, then there is no problem; he is entirely free to marry if he chooses, and he cannot be prevented. However undesirable or unsuitable this may seem to some people, there is nothing they can do to stop it. Their reasons may be good or bad, founded on logic or on prejudice, but the law will not support them if they try to prevent a marriage between two people who are of age and who understand what they are doing.

It is of course less simple in the case of mentally handicapped people. A person can only legally marry if he understands what marriage is. This does not mean that he must possess a full understanding of all the implications of marriage – what young couples do? It does mean, though, that he must know that he is committing himself, for life, to a union with someone of the opposite sex, to the exclusion of others. Even so, there are many handicapped people who would agree that this is what they intend (though not perhaps in such technical language) but who would not be able to handle the responsibilities that independent life, possibly with a baby, would involve. Common sense must be exercised: a mentally handicapped person to whom 'getting married' means dressing up, being applauded and kissed, living in a pretty home and holding a happy infant in one's arms, and nothing more, is obviously not ready to marry. No universal rule can be laid down which will deal with every situation in which mentally handicapped people say they want 'to get married', because the circumstances will differ in each case. Certainly, it is wise to discourage from marriage those who clearly cannot bring up a family, or at least to ensure that, if they do marry, there is no risk of pregnancy. How this is to be achieved in each individual case will depend on the people concerned, and of course on the professional advice available.

As this book is concerned with what will happen to a handicapped person after his parents have died, it is necessary to consider bereavement. One feeling that a handicapped child will certainly have, in common with children who are not handicapped, is great sadness, and a sense of bereavement and loss. He should be given as much preparation as possible for the fact that death comes to us all. His understanding is limited if he suffers from mental handicap, but nevertheless an attempt must be made to explain to him what death means. If this is not done, then he may feel, when the time comes, that he has been deserted by those who love him.

A discussion paper entitled *Bereavement and mentally handicapped people*, written by Maureen Oswin, has been published by the King's Fund Centre. The paper, which will be followed by a book based on detailed research by Miss Oswin, advances these principles:

1   There is no reason to think that people who are mentally handicapped will not go through stages of mourning, as do other people.
2   Mentally handicapped people have as much right as other people to be given consideration when their relatives and friends die.
3   Each person who is mentally handicapped is an individual, and will grieve as an individual; there is no reason to expect them to react in some particular way *because* they are mentally handicapped.
4   Some people who are mentally handicapped have particular disabilities, so they may need some special help when they become bereaved.

These principles are of course as applicable to those who have some other form of handicap as they are to mentally retarded people.

The paper *Bereavement and mentally handicapped people* gives the example of a mentally handicapped girl, Jane, who adjusted to her father's death because she was surrounded by caring people, went to his funeral, and was able to give extra help to her mother in the months that followed. She grieved for her father after his death, of course, but adjusted to the situation very well. Later, her mother died suddenly while Jane was out of the house during the day. The situation was unfortunately handled in a very different way: Jane was sent that night to a mental handicap hospital some twenty miles away from her home, although alternative arrangements were available, and a well-meaning relative kept her away from the funeral. Jane changed from being a secure, peaceful and happy woman to one whom the hospital staff described as 'anxious, sometimes aggressive and quarrelsome.' She then gradually became more passive and withdrawn.

No one had given Jane any chance to grieve for her mother, as she had been able to do for her father. Instead, she had been suddenly removed from her home and her friends on the very day that she lost her mother. An attempt, by the staff of the Training Centre that she used to attend, to visit Jane and talk about her mother's death, resulted in a telephone call from a social worker who said that 'the past should not be raked up'. We all need the chance to grieve and be comforted when someone we love has died. Handicapped people need this no less than the rest of us; they cannot be shielded from the fact of death. They will react, as Jane did, in different ways, depending on how they are treated.

Today's parents of handicapped children should help them understand the fact of death, and should help them grieve when other people die. More important than this, they should ensure that there will be someone ready and willing, when they die, to give immediate help and comfort to their bereaved son or daughter. Some parents are able to make financial provision for their children, others do not have money to leave; but all owe it to their children to see that they are helped to cope with bereavement when it comes.

In the next chapter, we shall consider the legal rights of handicapped people. It is very easy to ignore their human rights. If we pursue their legal entitlement to benefits and services with fervent zeal, there is a danger that we may forget that the happiness of a handicapped person depends on the quality of his life, far more than on the cash benefits which the State pays to him.

From her very considerable experience of working with handicapped people, Dr Joan Bicknell, who is Professor of the Psychiatry of Mental Handicap, London University, has analysed what she believes to be these human rights. Dr

Bicknell created one of the first Community Mental Handicap Teams in the country, a group of professionals with different skills whose task is to deal with all aspects of the life of mentally handicapped people in their area, to support their families, and to see that necessary services are provided. Dr Bicknell has suggested that any handicapped person has the right to take risks, to make choices and to take the consequences of his personal decisions. Most people, including the parents of a handicapped child, will accept this, but it creates some problems in practice. Is a young blind woman to be encouraged to make her way through the town, on public transport, if this is what she wants to do? Or is she to be dissuaded from doing this, and persuaded instead to go by car or taxi? If she does travel on public transport, can her parents accept the fact that she will meet people and form friendships with them? Many parents would be content for this to happen, provided they thought that the new friends were suitable. But what if they are not? This is a dilemma that all parents have, whether their child is handicapped or not; does the fact that the child is handicapped entitle them to decide that a particular friendship must come to an end? If so, how is their handicapped child to achieve independence, make mistakes and learn from them? Would their non-handicapped children allow parents to ban certain of their friends?

Dr Bicknell adds that a handicapped person has a right to work and to acquire leisure skills. At a time when paid employment is hard to find, it may be impossible for a handicapped person to earn money; but this does not mean that he can do nothing at all. He may be able, with training, to do a considerable amount of work in the home, and he will almost certainly enjoy leisure activities.

The right 'not to overburden their families, and in adulthood to be free from parental decision-making' and 'to leave home and live in ordinary housing' is far more difficult for parents to accept, yet it is proposed by Dr Bicknell. It has been her experience that, through the natural love and affection they bear their child, some parents keep him permanently dependent on them. Not only does this preserve him from stress and danger, but it also - over a period of time - gives his parents a sense of purpose. Dr Bicknell, in urging that a person who is handicapped should be free from the decision-making of his parents, is not criticising them. She is making proposals she feels are necessary for the benefit of the handicapped individual. Most parents will gladly admit that they would dearly like to see their handicapped child settled in a secure home at the time when they will themselves need care, by reason of sickness or old age. The difficulty may be to accept that this should happen earlier rather than later.

There is a need for self-advocacy by people who have a handicap. This is not a radical or an impractical idea. At national and international meetings it is now commonplace to hear both physically and mentally handicapped men and women say what they want. What stands out is that they wish to be treated as human beings, people with their own ambitions and interests. They say they want to live in ordinary houses, like the rest of us, and not in hospitals or institutions. They have a sense of humour, and they want to laugh. They do not want to be laughed at.

Philip is handicapped. He is spastic, and suffers from convulsions. He has a university degree and is now training for a professional career. He lives in a small community home where the house warden provides the essential minimum of services, but does not control the lives of the residents. Philip said:

I loved my parents, but they never wanted to let me go. Looking back, I see they treated me as a sort of household pet, not a person. They fed me, took me out in the car on weekends, and of course they loved me, but they wanted to keep me in a comfortable little room, cosseted and protected from the wicked world. In fact, the wicked world rather appeals to me, and when I am qualified I hope to work with a welfare rights organisation, and go into politics. If I get on the Council, they're going to have to make some changes to the Town Hall so that I can get up the stairs!

One can see that Philip is no household pet, but a real person, with a sense of humour and a lot of determination. There are others like him, some of whom are mentally handicapped, but who still have a mind of their own.

With normal children, it is recognised that they will leave home some time after their schooling is over. It gives their parents a new freedom, and usually lifts something of a financial burden as well. In cases where a child is handicapped, the time may come when they are dependent on him, not only in the personal and the emotional sense, but also financially. His Supplementary Benefit and other allowances may help to balance the family budget, especially when his parents have retired; but does this justify their keeping him at home long after he should have left to live his own life? Is he not, like other children, entitled to move out of his parents' house, into a home of his own?

Of course, suitable accommodation may not be easy to find. This is discussed in Chapter 8. Yet there are ways in which a permanent home can be found, and the parent who takes steps to see his child placed in one will be making sure that, when the time comes, he does not have to suffer both from bereavement and from a sudden move to an unsuitable place, all within a matter of days, as did Jane.

Hugh Card, a specialist social worker in the field of mental handicap with the East Sussex County Council, published the result of a survey he undertook, in 1983, in the area of the Eastbourne Health Authority. It was published in the magazine *Community Care* (July 28, 1983). Mr Card identified 131 families with a mentally handicapped child living at home, and sent a questionnaire to them. Almost 100 replied; the great majority said that they expected the Local Authority Social Services Department to provide a home for their child, but most had no idea what sort of accommodation would be available. Over 90% of the parents wanted to go on caring for their handicapped child until age or ill-health made this impossible, and many expressed great resentment against social workers who suggested short-term care and independence training for their children. The parents, for the most part, wanted their children to go into a staffed hostel eventually, but some were willing to have their children placed in a group home, a community village, or boarded out with a family. Several parents wrote of the self-sacrifice involved in looking after their handicapped child over many years, but rejected the suggestion that he or she should leave home before they, the parents, grew too old to provide care.

It was clear from Mr Card's survey that some parents were indeed relying on the State benefits, including Mobility and Attendance Allowances, to which their children were entitled, and that some of the children (though now adults) represented a focus for family activity and symbolised family unity. Many handicapped people were acting as baby-sitters and general domestic assistants. At times of illness in the family, mentally handicapped daughters were withdrawn from the Adult Training Centre which they were attending, to help care for a sick relative. The survey also found that, although parents appreciated the social skills that were taught in some Training Centres, it was unusual for this training to be continued or used within the family home. Parents stressed the limitations of their children, and the need for caution in pursuing independence. Mr Card says that he has the impression that parents' concern about the lack of residential provision in their areas is more an expression of their need for reassurance than a demand for an immediate service. He interviewed two handicapped women at an Adult Training Centre who told him there that they would like to leave their family home and live in a flat provided by the Local Council. However, when interviewed in their homes with their parents present, they said they wanted to remain at home.

Mr Card asks how far social workers should force the issue of independence with parents, and suggests that parents should see their child's departure from home as an important sacrifice – by the parents. In spite of the extent of his survey he does not seem to have picked up one major reason why parents are not willing to let their children leave home: the fact that they do not at all like the type of accommodation that the Local Authority is providing for handicapped people. There must be many parents who would be content to see their children in a good home while they, the parents, are still in good health, but who doubt whether the hostels and group homes in their area are adequate. In spite of this omission, there is much in Mr Card's survey that cannot be dismissed, and parents will do well to consider whether a move might really be in their child's interests, and would enable him to live his own life, independent of them.

To return to the suggestions made by Dr Bicknell, she advocates that handicapped people should not only be encouraged to leave home, if the right place is available, but that they should be allowed to make friendships, and to have privacy, an opportunity for personal achievement, and a chance to exercise their sexuality. She makes the point that a handicapped person will probably be taken by bus to school or to a Training Centre some way from home, and that it will therefore be difficult for him to make new friendships. All the more reason for him to join a leisure club near home, if possible where there are non-handicapped people as well as those with handicap. Privacy, too, is important. Some handicapped people live in a room into which anyone feels they can walk whenever they wish. 'How often', asks Dr Bicknell, 'do we see the bedroom door of a handicapped person opened without any knocking, and how frequently are visitors trailed round our units and shown every nook and cranny without any thought for the fact that this is someone's substitute home?' She is writing of life in a hostel, but her remarks apply equally to many people who are living at home with their parents.

There will be some who read these views and who will feel that professionals are all too eager to lecture parents on their responsibilities, but that they do not know what it is really like to care for a handicapped child from birth to middle-age. It imposes a heavy burden on parents, and prevents them from living a life like others can do. The fact of their child's handicap may prevent parents from going out in the evenings; it will govern the type of holiday they can take; and it may restrict their lives in a hundred ways. What right, they may ask, have professors, social workers and professional people – including authors – to tell them how they should carry their burden?

To this question there is no easy answer. No professional person has the right to assume that he knows best. He may be able to advise; he may have additional technical knowledge; he may think that a client, or a patient, is making a mistake – and he may be right. On the other hand, he may be wrong. The object of the professional must be to give the best advice he can, and, just as important, to understand the feelings of parents. In fact, it is the parents' feelings that will govern what they do. All the advice in the world will not convince the parent who is determined that his child is not going to leave home, and that he knows best.

It is the same with a book: it cannot change the mind of someone who is going to pursue a particular course of action, come what may. For this reason, the suggestions made in the remaining chapters are put forward as a series of options which parents and relatives of handicapped people may adopt, if they see fit. It is often they who will decide what style of life the handicapped person will be allowed to enjoy.

3 Legal Rights and State Benefits

The law starts with the assumption that everyone has the same rights, and the same responsibilities, whether or not they are handicapped. To give examples, in the eyes of the law, a handicapped person can own property, get married and commit a crime, unless it is shown that he is incapable of understanding what these things involve. Many handicapped people have no particular difficulty in understanding the law; though confined to a bed, or a wheelchair, there is no reason at all why they should not own property, or make contracts with other people. Only at the moment when a handicapped person cannot understand what ownership means, or is behaving irrationally, may he be deprived of the usual rights of ownership. Unfortunately, the families of many handicapped people do not consider them fit to manage money or other property, simply because they cannot move about the place, or have some mild form of mental handicap. Such attitudes simply go to create a greater incapacity and result in the almost complete dependence of the handicapped person on the people around him.

The parent who accepts that the day will come when he or she can no longer care for a handicapped child should take every possible step to help him manage things for himself. Mrs Black had a son, Eric, who was diagnosed as mildly mentally handicapped. She was ashamed of his condition, but loved him deeply and was very protective. Apart from going to school and later to an Adult Training Centre, Eric was never allowed out, unless of course he was with her. She did not take him into shops but they did work in the garden together, and sometimes she took him for walks. He managed his own toilet, but she chose all his clothes and always dressed him. She even cut up his food so that he could eat it without difficulty. She refused to let him go to a nearby leisure club; the organisers offered to pick him up in a bus and bring him back home, but she was worried about what might happen to him there and did not let him go. She had heard that they sometimes went away on trips to the seaside and the country, but she decided that there would be danger for him there. She was probably right: having never been taught to do anything for himself, Eric would have found it very difficult to cope with the freedom of unfamiliar surroundings.

Mrs Black had to go into hospital for a thyroid operation, and her husband could not stay away from work for the long period of her convalescence. Eric went to a short-stay home run by the Social Services Department of the County Council. There he was encouraged to do far more things for himself, and he learned to go on public transport, with the other residents, to an Adult Training Centre. When his mother came out of hospital she found a rather different Eric; he wanted to dress himself and was angry when she touched his food. He had been given some spending money at the home, and had bought several ties which he insisted on wearing. He also said that he wanted to continue at the Adult Training Centre where the staff had found him a quick learner and were recommending him for an Industrial Training Unit. Even more worrying from his mother's point of view was that he now had a girl friend. He had learnt how to use the telephone, and he wanted to call her each evening.

It is very easy to blame Mrs Black and others like her. It is she who has accepted the very real burden of coping with a child who is intellectually handicapped. Her care and her love have protected him and made him feel secure. The time has now come, however, for her to plan for the day when she will no longer be able to do everything for him. If she goes on as she did before her operation, Eric may one day find himself in surroundings that are wholly unsuitable for him, unhappy and lonely. If she can now begin to let go, encourage him to do things for himself, attend the Adult Training Centre, see his girl friend and go to the leisure club, she will be giving him the chance to prepare for that part of his life that he is going to have to live without her. If she takes no steps to prepare him for this, she may be condemning him to a much less happy existence. The way he has lived until now has led him to believe that people will do things for him; but that is not how the world works outside his home. The more he can learn to do for himself, the better his life will be when he is on his own.

The same principles apply to the State Benefits to which Eric is entitled. Steps should be taken now to ensure that he is receiving everything that he should, and that he knows how to manage what he is given, to the best of his ability. His parents should, if possible, claim his benefits and establish his right to them so that, when he is on his own, he will not miss out. There are many thousands of handicapped and elderly people who do not claim State Benefits simply because they, or the people caring for them, do not know of their existence. Some families do not make claims because they feel the benefits are a form of charity which they would rather not accept. They are entitled to this view for themselves, but it may harm their handicapped child in time to come, leaving him short of the money he needs.

Later chapters in this book discuss property rights, but we shall deal here with State Benefits, and with some of the legal responsibilities, and liabilities, of handicapped people. These are the main benefits to which a handicapped person may be entitled, and which should be claimed for him or her:

Attendance Allowance
Mobility Allowance (and Road Tax Refund)
Rate Relief and Rates Rebate
Rent Rebates and Allowances
Reduced Fares

Invalid Care Allowance
Family Income Supplement
Special Services
Non-Contributory Invalidity Pension
Supplementary Benefit and Additions

There are various other allowances which families may claim if they are looking after a handicapped child, but we shall not consider these here, as we are concerned with those benefits that will continue to be available to the handicapped person when he is no longer living at home with his parents.

ATTENDANCE ALLOWANCE

This allowance is for people who need to be looked after because they have a physical or mental disability. If a child is to receive the allowance, he must be in need of more care than average children. A deaf child, for example, qualifies automatically. Parents can claim the allowance from the time when their child is two years old, and there is no upper age limit. The allowance itself belongs to the handicapped person (even to a young child), but is often collected by his parent or someone else, and spent on his behalf. Claims are made on Form NI 205.

In order to decide whether a child or an older handicapped person requires extra care and attention, a statement by the parent and a medical report by a doctor will be needed. The doctor's examination takes place at home, and it is not done by the family's general practitioner, but by a doctor specially appointed by the Department of Health and Social Security. The doctor will usually take down the parent's statement and ask him or her to sign it. It is a good idea to write a note, the night before the visit from the doctor, of all that requires to be done for your handicapped child. A useful check-list can be obtained from the Disability Alliance (see Appendix IV). You can use this to make sure that you miss out nothing important. Make sure that, after the examination is over and the doctor has written down his notes of what has been said, he has included all your points; you should do this before you sign the statement.

Some parents feel that they are letting down their child by giving details of all the things that he cannot do for himself and all the problems from which he suffers. In a way, they feel that this is disloyal to him. It is not. If he is entitled, because of his disability, to receive the Attendance Allowance, then of course it should be paid to him, and used for his benefit. If this does not happen, financial hardship may later deny him the chance to lead a full life and to make progress towards greater independence. So the list to be given to the doctor should be as full as possible. He will never have met the handicapped child before, and the information about what has to be done for him is exactly what the Attendance Board needs to supplement the doctor's assessment. He will send his own medical report, together with your statement, to the Board, which then makes up its mind on whether the Allowance should be paid, and if so at what rate.

The conditions for being given the Allowance are known as the 'Day Conditions' and the 'Night Conditions'. A higher rate will be paid if both the Day and the Night Conditions apply. The Day Conditions are that the disabled person requires *either* frequent attention throughout the day in connection with his bodily functions, e.g. toilet, washing and eating, *or* continual supervision throughout the day in order to avoid substantial danger to himself or to others. The Night Conditions are similar but not exactly the same. They are that the disabled person requires either 'prolonged or repeated attention' during the night in connection with his bodily functioning, or continual supervision throughout the night to avoid substantial danger to himself or to others. Whether the higher rate is paid depends on whether attention is needed day and night, not on the actual degree of disability.

The Attendance Allowance Board issues a certificate of entitlement to the Allowance, and this may say that it will be payable only for a limited number of years, after which it can be renewed if there has been another medical examination. A further examination often takes place at age sixteen, when the disabled person starts to receive the Supplementary Benefit, the Non-Contributory Invalidity Pension, or both. There has been an increasing tendency in recent years for the Attendance Allowance Unit to require this review at age sixteen or eighteen, a policy which may have resulted from the Government's attempt to save taxpayers' money. However, if a handicapped person qualifies for the Allowance, it should most certainly be claimed. If he still requires the extra attention, the fact that he can now claim other Benefits is irrelevant. Failure to claim, or to contest a decision to withdraw the Allowance, may deprive the handicapped person of a good deal of money, over a long period of time. The Allowance is not a taxable benefit, and it does not reduce the amount of any other benefit that may be payable. It is not paid for children living in hospitals, boarding schools or Local Authority Homes. It *is* payable during visits home, so parents should establish their child's entitlement and then claim for the periods he spends at home. Conversely, in the case of a child living at home but spending periods in a hospital or a Home, parents should inform the DHSS, which will stop the Allowance for any week in which the child spends four or more days away from home. Adults going into a hospital or a Home will only lose the Allowance after four weeks have expired.

Doreen Bassett was receiving the Attendance Allowance at the lower rate. When she reached sixteen years, it was withdrawn. The local office of the DHSS was told by Doreen's mother that she was now able to go to school using public transport, and they thought (quite wrongly, as it turned out) that this meant she should no longer have the Allowance. Her mother asked for the case to be 'reviewed'. A review is in practice a form of appeal, and can be requested within three months of a decision that the Allowance is to be stopped. Mrs Bassett pointed out that Doreen was still not able to wash herself properly, either after eating or going to the toilet, and that she had started wandering round the house at night. During these nocturnal walks, she had been known to try to push electric fires into the wrong sockets, and to light the gas oven in the kitchen. There was a real danger that she might burn the house down. After another specially appointed doctor had been to see her, and had noted everything that Mrs Bassett said to him, her appeal on behalf of Doreen was successful. The Allowance was restored, this time at the higher rate.

In Doreen's case, new circumstances had arisen (her night-time wanderings) which made a change in the rate of the Attendance Allowance that was payable to her. The same would be true if a disabled person deteriorated and, after a period of being able to cope on her own, had to receive extra care. Anyone making an application for review on behalf of the person entitled to benefit should obtain letters from those who can provide useful evidence. In Mrs Bassett's case, she was able to persuade Doreen's teacher to write a note confirming that she could not clean herself after using the toilet at school. The family doctor was able to report that he had been prescribing medicines for Doreen, to help her sleep a little better, but without much success.

When a review takes place, copies of the doctor's report and of any supporting letters are sent to the claimant, or to the person responsible for caring for him. In Doreen's case, if this had omitted any important factor, or had shown that Doreen's condition had been misunderstood, Mrs Bassett could have pointed this out to the Board. She succeeded in her appeal on the review. If she had failed she could have gone to the Local Appeals Tribunal, provided she did this within 28 days of receiving notice of the Board's decision. The Tribunal has no power to make medical decisions, because this is always left to the doctor who has examined the disabled person, but it can over-rule the Board on any question relating to the inter-pretation of the Regulations. It would have had the power, for example, to say that the fact that Doreen could travel on a bus was irrelevant to the question of her entitlement to the Allowance.

Parents who are dissatisfied with a decision made by the Board, or by the Tribunal, can appeal - on a point of law - to a Social Security Commissioner. They should first consult one of the welfare organisations whose names and addresses are given in Appendix IV of this book. They can, of course, also obtain a solicitor's advice. After the claimant has reached the age of sixteen, and certainly if he is receiving Supplementary Benefit, legal advice will be available under the Legal Aid and Advice Scheme. (See Chapter 4). There is an ultimate appeal from the Commissioner, but this is a step that should be taken only with the help and advice of a solicitor.

MOBILITY ALLOWANCE

The Mobility Allowance is intended to make it possible for disabled people to get out more than they could otherwise do. It recognises that they may have to pay more for cars, taxis, escorts and equipment which is not available from the National Health Service. The Allowance can be claimed between the ages of five and sixty-five, and claims are accepted up to the sixtieth birthday. If the Allowance is being paid at age sixty-five, then it will continue to seventy-five. Claims are made on Form NI 211.

Unlike the Attendance Allowance, the Mobility Allowance can be paid to people who are living in hospitals and in Local Authority Homes. The claimant must be capable of benefiting from the increase in mobility which payment of the Allowance will make possible. In practice, this excludes very few people, because even the most severely handicapped can benefit from a change in their surroundings, from sea air and sunshine. The Allowance can be paid to another person who has been nominated to draw it on behalf of the handicapped person. If he lives at home this will normally be a relative, but if not it may be the hospital administrator or the Local Authority in whose Home he is living. The DHSS does not make any check on how the Allowance is spent once it has been awarded, but the regulations are clear that it must be spent for the benefit of the individual to whom it is awarded. There have been cases in which family members, or others, have used the money for themselves and not for the handicapped person. This is legally wrong, and in some circumstances can even be criminal.

The money paid by way of Mobility Allowance must not be pooled with money belonging to other people, and Statutory Authorities are advised by the DHSS to keep separate accounts for each person. Mobility Allowance is not taxed, nor is it offset against any other benefits.

To qualify for the Mobility Allowance a claimant has to show that he is 'unable or virtually unable to walk' by reason of 'physical' disablement. He will normally have to undergo a medical examination in order to establish this. The examination will be arranged to take place as near to his home as possible, and it will be carried out by a specially appointed doctor. You can request a home visit if it would be too difficult to attend somewhere else.

The words 'unable or virtually unable to walk' have been defined in this way: '. . . if his ability to walk out of doors is so limited, as regards the distance over which or the speed at which or the length of time for which or the manner in which he can make progress on foot without severe discomfort, that he is virtually unable to walk.' A claimant will also qualify if the exertion of walking would endanger his life, or lead to a serious deterioration in his health. Any special aids which the handicapped person usually wears should be worn at the medical examination.

A careful reading of the above paragraphs will indicate the points which you should make, and which the doctor should include in his notes. As with an application for the Attendance Allowance, you should make your notes the day before the examination takes place. It will be worth measuring the distance your child can walk without suffering acute discomfort. You can also work out the speed at which he gets along, though this can be more difficult and needs to be measured over, say, a quarter of a mile i.e. over 400 yards. This is linked, of course, with the amount of time he takes to cover the distance. The way in which he progresses should also be noted. Does he keep his balance and is he able to go in a particular direction? Does he feel pain? Can he walk without help from someone else? As the Mobility Allowance is intended to help your child with outdoor mobility, ask the doctor to make his observations outside the house.

If the application for the Allowance is turned down, you can appeal, within 28 days, to a Medical Board on medical grounds, or to an Appeal Tribunal on other grounds. The reasons for your appeal must of course be stated. Unlike the appeal for an Attendance Allowance, that for the Mobility Allowance involves attending before a Board of doctors. You should keep the notes you originally made for the first doctor, and add anything that you may have missed out. Letters supporting your case, from the family doctor, a social worker, a teacher or some other professional person who knows your child, will be useful. A teacher, for example, might be able to write that your child suffers from chest pains if he has to walk some distance in the playground at school, or that he often has to use a wheelchair when the class goes across the road to the Park, because he walks so very slowly. It is good practice to send copies of a letter of this kind, with your own statement of appeal.

If the decision of the Medical Board is unsatisfactory, it is still possible to make an appeal to a Medical Appeal Tribunal. This must be made within three months. If this appeal fails, then it is possible to appeal yet again - within three months of the Tribunal's decision - to a National Insurance Commissioner. This appeal, however, has to be on a point of law. In this process of making appeals you will certainly need some help, either from a welfare organisation or from a solicitor. Do not forget that your child may himself qualify for Legal Aid and Advice, even if you do not. A good welfare rights organisation is invaluable in co-ordinating the roles of yourself, your solicitor and any other person who is concerned professionally with your child. The statements of everyone concerned will concentrate on the central issues of the appeal. As a last resort there may be an appeal to the courts, but this should only take place on legal advice.

Anyone receiving the Supplementary Benefit will be given free Legal Aid and Advice. About 70 per cent of the population is in fact entitled to Legal Aid, but some people will have to make a contribution towards its cost. The amount of the contribution depends on one's 'disposable income' and 'disposable capital'. If you have a disposable income of more than £1,850 a year, then you will have to make a contribution, the amount of which rises as your income goes up. The same principle applies to someone with disposable capital of more than £1,300. It should not be assumed that Legal Aid is only available to very poor people. A single man earning as much as £6,721 a year, or a married man with three children earning £11,511 a year, may both be eligible.

Many parents are discouraged from making appeals against the decisions of Boards and Tribunals, because life for them is already difficult enough. Mr and Mrs Drake took their daughter's case to a Tribunal, and finally on to a court; they could not have afforded to do this on their own, but Legal Aid made all the difference. Their daughter's application for the Mobility Allowance had been turned down because she could in fact walk. However, she had no sense of direction and was not mobile in any real sense. She could move about easily enough, but might set off in the wrong direction, or turn back after only a few moments. Only with help could she make any sort of progress. Unfortunately, the Drakes lost the appeal; it was decided, as a matter of law, that their daughter was not 'unable or virtually unable to walk', even though she was incapable of getting from one place to another without constant help. Many people have been harmed by this unfortunate decision, and voluntary organisations are bringing political pressure to have the law changed, for it does not seem to make sense at present. In spite of this, it may still be worthwhile for parents to go ahead with appeals to a Tribunal, because about one third of them do in fact succeed.

Anyone receiving the Mobility Allowance can also claim refund of the Road Tax, which is a valuable benefit for anyone who can only travel around in a special vehicle. Help on all problems of Mobility is available from the organisation Motability (see Appendix IV). Any disabled person who receives the Mobility Allowance can of course continue to claim it after his parents have died.

OTHER BENEFITS AND ALLOWANCES

Rate Relief and Rates Rebate
Rate relief can be claimed by people who have paid for alterations or additions at home to make life easier for a handicapped person. Rates Rebates may also be available, but they depend on family income and circumstances. They can be back-dated for a year, so it is worth making a claim if you think you may be entitled to them. At your local Council offices there is a leaflet *Rate Relief for Disabled Persons*, which explains the Rebates and how to claim them.

Rent Rebates and Allowances
Some families can obtain a reduction in the rent they pay for their home, or can apply for an extra allowance to help them pay their rent. Another leaflet, entitled *There's Money off the Rent*, can be obtained from the local Council.

Reduced Fares
These may be available for travel on public transport. Several handicapped people go to and from Adult Training Centres on buses; details of reduced fares are available at the bus depot or the railway station.

Invalid Care Allowance
Relatives can claim this Allowance if they are looking after someone receiving the Attendance Allowance. A man can claim if he has to stay at home to do this. A woman can claim if she is on her own, and is not receiving maintenance payments from her husband.

Family Income Supplement
There are some families with a handicapped child who are on a low income, and they can can claim this payment if the person claiming is in full-time work, or is self-employed and working for at least 30 hours a week (24 hours for a single person). The amount of the Supplement depends on the family's income.

These rebates, allowances and supplements are mentioned here because it is quite possible that a handicapped person may be cared for by another member of the family after his parents have died or have become too old to look after him. It is important that the claims should be made long before this happens, to ensure that they will continue to be paid, uninterrupted, when a change takes place.

SPECIAL SERVICES
People who have a permanent and substantial handicap may register as disabled under the Chronically Sick and Disabled Persons Act 1970. The handicap from which they suffer can be physical or mental, or both, but it must be permanent. Registration is through the local Social Services Department, which has a duty to try to obtain various items and services for the handicapped individual. These can include:

Help with travelling arrangements
Holidays
Adaptations to the home
Meals at home, or elsewhere

A telephone
Radio, television, a library or similar recreation
Practical assistance, for example, a Home Help

Some handicapped people may be required to make a contribution towards the cost of these services, but not if their only resource is the Supplementary Benefit. There is unfortunately a considerable variation throughout the country in the willingness of Local Authorities to provide this help, but they certainly will not do so unless they are asked. Families with a handicapped member should apply for registration on his behalf, or of course he may be able to do it for himself. The benefits he receives may continue for the rest of his life.

NON-CONTRIBUTORY INVALIDITY PENSION (NCIP)

This Pension provides an income for people who are unable to work because of a disability, but who have no record of National Insurance contributions which would normally entitle them to a pension. It is not paid to a married woman, unless she is incapable of doing housework. From the age of 16, it is payable to all handicapped people who can provide a medical certificate stating that they have been incapable of work for the previous 28 weeks. The doctor must state a time limit for the incapacity, and it is sometimes necessary to ask him for more certificates as time goes by. However, the doctor may be willing to use the word 'indefinitely' on the certificate, meaning that the handicapped person will never be able to work because of his disability.

The Non-Contributory Invalidity Pension, which you will hear referred to as the 'NCIP', is payable even if the handicapped person is still at school or college, but when it begins to be paid the parent will no longer be entitled to receive the Child Benefit. The NCIP can be claimed, using Form NI 210, at any time between the ages of 16 and 65 for a man, and up to 60 for a woman. After these ages, the payment will continue if the person is not entitled to a Retirement Pension, or if such a pension would be less than the NCIP. There is no means test for the NCIP which can be a great advantage if the handicapped person has money of his own, or if there exists a trust in his favour. There is further detailed information about the situation in Chapter 6. Parents will find that in most circumstances it is beneficial to their child to apply for the NCIP on his behalf, at least from the moment when they no longer receive the Child Benefit. Once it is being paid, then it is most unlikely to be withdrawn, whereas payments of Supplementary Benefit may suddenly cease if the claimant becomes entitled to money or other property.

Severe Disablement Allowance
The Government recently announced plans for a new Social Security Benefit, to be called the Severe Disablement Allowance. It will replace the Non-Contributory Invalidity Pension and will be payable from November 1984. It will initially be at the same rate as the NCIP, which in November 1983 was raised to £20.45. The new Allowance will be payable to:

1   Those already incapable of work by the age of 20, on a simple test of that incapacity.
2   Those becoming incapable of work after that age, if they are also 80 per cent or more disabled by reference to the measure of loss or faculty successfully used in the industrial injuries and war pensions schemes.
3   All existing recipients of Non-Contributory Invalidity Pension.

SUPPLEMENTARY BENEFIT
As soon as a handicapped person reaches the age of 16, he can claim Supplementary Benefit in his own right, regardless of his parents' 'means', that is, of their income and the property they own. This Benefit is intended to bring everyone up to a minimum living standard, and it can be paid to handicapped

people who are still at school, provided that, even if they were available for work, they would be unlikely to get it, owing to their disability. The Benefit is claimed on National Insurance Form SB 1, and starts at a basic rate. This rate is increased after a year to the Long Term Rate, and then goes up – at age 18 – to the Adult Rate. Normally, the Government increases the amount of the Benefit each year, in the month of November, to keep pace with inflation. A married woman cannot claim the Supplementary Benefit in her own right, but if her husband is entitled to it, he can claim extra for her as a dependant.

There is nothing to prevent a handicapped person from applying for some Supplementary Benefit, as well as for the NCIP. For most handicapped people, it makes very good sense to do this, and parents whose children are only receiving Supplementary Benefit should consider applying for NCIP, with a 'top-up' payment by way of Benefit. When this is done, there is the advantage that the handicapped person is being paid the non-means-tested NCIP, and may also be entitled to some additional payments, over and above the basic Supplementary Benefit Rate. The most common of these 'Additions' are:

The Rent Addition
This is payable to people over the age of 18, who are living at home with their family. If they are living in their own accommodation, then their rent will normally be paid for them.

The Heating Addition
This is payable automatically to all those who are being paid Supplementary Benefit and who also receive the Attendance Allowance or the Mobility Allowance, and it is also given to some others with specific physical additions. The Heating Addition is claimed on Form OC 2. If there is a problem in paying heating bills, there is a useful Code of Practice sheet at local gas and electricity showrooms.

The Diet Addition
This is an extra payment that varies according to need. A certificate from a doctor will usually be needed before it can be claimed.

The Clothing Addition
This will be paid for extra wear and tear on clothes which is due to the disability.

The Bath Addition
This is payable for baths above one per week, taken for health reasons. It is especially useful for those handicapped people who are incontinent.

It is appropriate to stress again the good sense of applying for both the NCIP and the Supplementary Benefit. Because the Benefit is means-tested, its amount is reduced by the weekly NCIP payment, and by the amount of some other income sources, though not by the amount of Attendance Allowance or Mobility Allowance. All parents should apply for the NCIP for their handicapped child after he reaches the age of 16, as it will provide a steady income, even if the child inherits money. It does sometimes happen that a grandparent leaves money to be divided equally among his grandchildren, not realising the complications that will result. See Chapters 6 and 7 for full details of these, and Chapter 9 on some ways of avoiding the difficulties. If a child does inherit money, however, although the Supplementary Benefit may cease to be payable, the NCIP will continue undisturbed, and there will be no great change in the child's situation. This is yet another example of a situation where inaction by parents can harm a child's interests.

Of course, it is easier to ignore the NCIP, and just make the claim for the Supplementary Benefit, and Mrs Clarke did this. She collected the full Supplementary Benefit for her daughter Beryl for many years. Then she died after a short illness, without having troubled to make a will. 'It will all go to Beryl anyway,' she used to tell her friends. After a certain amount of trouble and a great deal of delay, caused by the fact that she died intestate, Beryl became entitled to everything, including Mrs Clarke's small terrace house. As a result, Beryl immediately ceased to receive any Supplementary Benefit, which was withdrawn. A relative took her into her home, but she could not keep her there permanently, especially as Beryl was proving a financial burden. The relative had never heard of the NCIP, and as Mrs Clarke had never claimed it for her daughter, it was of course not being paid, even though she was entitled to it.

It was months before the house could be sold; a Grant of Letters of Administration to Mrs Clarke's Estate had to be obtained, and an application had also to be made to the Court of Protection because of Beryl's ownership of property. (See Chapter 7.) Everything went very slowly, and the relative who was caring for Beryl grew fed up with the situation and with the drain on her own income. This increased her unwillingness to continue to keep Beryl, who realised what was happening and began to be very fearful about her future. Mrs Clarke's inaction, due of course to the fact that she did not know about claiming the NCIP or making a will, made things much worse for Beryl. A social worker advised the relative about a claim for NCIP, but by this time the situation had deteriorated, the relative had become angry at what had happened, and was feeling that, with all Beryl's money available (though not yet paid), something ought to be given to her to compensate her for the expense to which she had been put, and the trouble of looking after Beryl. She told the social worker that she was no longer willing to look after Beryl, who had to leave. If she had been receiving the NCIP before her mother's death, and if her mother had made a will, much of this uncertainty and distress could have been prevented.

The law may affect handicapped people in various other ways, for example in relation to:

Employment
Contracts
Tax
Education
Voting
Crime
Sexual offences

We shall deal with these separately, always remembering that
the law starts with the assumption that handicapped people
have the same legal rights and responsibilities as everyone else.

EMPLOYMENT

Many physically and mentally handicapped people are holding
down a job, full or part-time. Within the past fifteen years, new
laws have been passed which have given all employees new
rights, and these apply especially if they have been made redundant, or have been dismissed. They apply fully to handicapped
people, just as to anyone else. Anyone who becomes employed
is entering into a legal contract with his employer. This
contract is binding on him, provided he understands what he is
doing when he starts work. A physically disabled employee is
therefore in no better and no worse position than any other
worker. If he is made redundant, or is dismissed in an unfair
manner, then he will be entitled to compensation. In particular,
if his dismissal is both unfair and due to his disability, he will
have a substantial claim for damages against his employer. Of
course, if his disability worsens or causes him to be unable to
continue to do his job properly, then the dismissal may be fair;
it all depends on the particular circumstances of each case.

A mentally handicapped person may not be able to understand the nature of his contract, in which case he is not legally
bound by its terms. On the other hand, if he knows that he must
turn up on time, cannot leave until a specified hour, must work
while he is at the shop, factory or hotel where he is employed,
must do what he is told by the manager or foreman, and that in

return for his work he will be regularly paid, then he understands enough to enter into a legally binding contract of employment. He is not expected to know all about employment law, any more than most people do.

The Royal Society for Mentally Handicapped Children and Adults (Mencap) runs an employment service, known as the Pathway Scheme. This is now operating in many parts of the country, and is described in more detail in Chapter 4. There are many employers who now have working for them mentally handicapped people with whom they are totally satisfied and whom they pay the standard wage. One employer in Cardiff was so pleased with the work done by a young man that he asked the Mencap Pathway Scheme to send him two more people. The young man working for him turned up on time, he said, even in the worst weather; he never left early, always did what he was asked, and did not find repetitive jobs uninteresting. There was no difficulty with other employees, one of whom had been appointed, by Mencap, to make sure that all was well, and who received a small fee for his trouble.

The Pathway Scheme involves a special payment by Mencap to the employer to cover the first period of employment, as some businesses are uncertain whether they want to take the risk of taking on a mentally handicapped person. If the situation is satisfactory to both employer and employee, it then continues on a permanent basis. Problems do of course arise from time to time, but the Pathway Officer is available to sort them out. Parents whose children may be able to work should find out whether this Scheme is operating in their own area.

CONTRACTS

A contract is a legally binding arrangement between two people, or perhaps between organisations. One person makes an offer which the other accepts, and there is also agreement over the price, known to lawyers as the 'consideration'. The subject of the contract may be an item of goods, for example a trolley full of items in a supermarket, or a service, such as an adjustment to a faulty television set. Every purchase in a shop, every ticket bought on a bus, a train or an aircraft, involves a contract, as does an insurance policy, a hire purchase agreement or even a house purchase. A contract is binding on a handicapped person, as already explained, unless it can be shown that he did not understand what he was doing when he entered into it, and the other person was aware, or should have been aware, of his incapacity.

To give an example, if a mentally handicapped woman offered a shop-keeper a 50p piece and took a chocolate bar worth 30p from the counter, then accepted 20p change and left the shop with the bar, this would be a perfectly legal contract. She would not be legally entitled to change her mind and get her money back, although it is possible that the shop-keeper might let her do this, or might allow her to take some other item of the same value. On the other hand, if the handicapped woman had entered a shop selling high-fidelity radio equipment, and said that she wanted an expensive machine, it would quickly become apparent that she was of only limited understanding and did not really appreciate the implications of what she was doing. If she handed over some money and then signed a hire-purchase agreement, without any real understanding of its meaning, the contract (and the HP agreement) would not be binding on her. Indeed, the shop-keeper would be taking a stupid risk in such circumstances, and would almost certainly have to bear any cost that resulted from damage to the machine. Even if the shop-keeper said that he did not know that the woman was mentally handicapped, a court would probably decide that he should have known, because it was obvious from her behaviour, and the legal position would be the same. There are of course border-line cases which are difficult to decide, but a salesman who is eager to sell his product should always be careful if his customer seems to be handicapped. Fortunately, the law now allows a 'cooling-off' period in the case of many (not all) agreements, and there is usually an opportunity to cancel an unwise arrangement.

TAX

A handicapped person with an income will have to pay tax, provided of course his income reaches the level at which it is payable. In assessing his liability his NCIP will be taken into account, but not the Attendance Allowance or the Mobility Allowance. He is equally liable to pay Value Added Tax if he is supplied with goods or services. If he possesses substantial property, then the law concerning Capital Gains Tax and Capital Transfer Tax will apply to him. He may need professional advice to enable him to minimise the amount of tax payable; if his handicap is physical and not mental, this will present no difficulty, but mentally handicapped people may require special help. This can be obtained on their behalf by their family, and in particular by a guardian (for someone under 18) or by a receiver appointed by the Court of Protection. There is more on this subject in Chapter 7. It may be appropriate for the parents of a handicapped person to apply to the Court of Protection, during their own lives, so that their child's property can be properly administered during their lifetime, and of course after they have died. If this is to be done, then the help of a solicitor is essential.

EDUCATION

Since 1971, all handicapped people have been entitled to an education. The Local Education Authority may allocate them a place in a Special School, or possibly in an ordinary Primary or Secondary School, depending on their needs. The Education Authority is legally obliged, by the Education Act 1981, to identify all children with special education needs, and must assess these. It will then produce a statement which the parents must be allowed to see. Parents are legally entitled to know about the decisions that are made about their child's future, and they must be consulted. Mentally handicapped children will normally receive an education from age 2, including those who are in hospital. They can continue to receive education up to their nineteenth birthday, provided it can be shown that this will benefit them. There are very few cases indeed where a young man or woman cannot benefit at all from education between the ages of 16 and 19, even if he or she is mentally handicapped. Parents can insist that they receive it. The technical legal aspects of this are discussed in Appendix II. If parents experience difficulty they should obtain legal advice, or ask for help from the Regional Office of Mencap, the address of which is given in Appendix IV.

Parents should also consider making an application to the Local Education Authority for financial support to enable their child to receive further education. A grant or an award may be made, and other forms of financial support. For example, there are training establishments run especially for handicapped people who have recently left school. The courses run for two years or more; handicapped students live and work at the establishments, supported by grants from Local Education Authorities. A normal child of good intelligence is entitled to a grant for university education, and there are many Education Authorities who are willing to give a similar grant to enable a handicapped person to receive appropriate further education. Handicapped people who are living in the community, or in institutional establishments, may also take advantage of adult education services. Parents, working together, can bring pressure on the Education Authority to provide these services for their handicapped children, and this can have a profound and beneficial effect on their future life.

It is vitally important that parents should ensure that their children receive the maximum education to which they are entitled; this will help them to achieve the greatest degree of independence they can attain, and will give them the opportunity for a full life. Without opportunities of this kind, their handicap is made worse, because of their total dependence on their parents. However well cared for they may be while their parents are still alive, education will help them to cope with life in the years to come. This education need not be academic; social education is available which can equip handicapped people to live effectively and happily in the community, or in a suitable home.

VOTING

When we reach the age of 18 we are entitled to vote, and handicapped people are no exception. They must of course first have their names entered on the electoral roll, and when the moment to vote arrives they must be able to confirm that they are the person whose name is on the register of electors. One's name is placed on the register for a Parliamentary constituency and for a Local Government Ward, on the basis of residence. All physically handicapped people should certainly be entered on a register, and so should those mentally handicapped men and women who know how to vote, and understand what they are doing.

CRIME

Unfortunately, mentally handicapped people sometimes find themselves in trouble with the police. Mr and Mrs Draper were horrified one evening when they received a telephone call from the local police station, saying that their son Robert had been charged with breaking and entering a factory, with intent to steal goods that had been stored there. Immediately they went to the police station, where they found that Robert had already confessed to a crime, and had signed a statement to say that he had done it. Apparently, the police had been called by an alert neighbour, but the rest of the gang of teenagers had run away when they heard the police car coming. Robert had not run away; he did not really understand what was happening, though he thought it was all quite fun. He was found standing by a stolen packing-case, just inside the factory gate, the lock on which had been forced. In answer to the questions of the police, he said that he had 'seen Bill break the lock', and that he had gone inside to see if there was anything interesting there. He had also answered 'Yes' to several other questions that the police had asked, because this was what he usually did.

Robert went home with his parents who told the police that he was mentally handicapped. At first, they seemed very doubtful about this, because in many ways he appeared to be normal. He went to an ordinary comprehensive school, and this made them even more suspicious. They asked why he was not at a Special School, if he was handicapped. In fact, the Local Education Authority had placed him in the comprehensive because it was thought that he could benefit from contact with other young people. It was some of them, of course, who had led him to involvement in the burglary. Mr and Mrs Draper went to see their solicitor the next day; the family doctor was able to confirm that Robert was intellectually handicapped, and his parents told the police, at the solicitor's suggestion, that he was a member of the local Gateway Club. These Clubs cater for young and not-so-young people with mental handicap. There are more than 600 of them throughout the country, and they are well known to the police, who understand and support their work. The fact that Robert Draper belonged to the Gateway Club was what finally persuaded the police that he probably did not really know what he was doing when he joined the other boys who were breaking into the factory. They therefore did not proceed with charges against Robert, which were withdrawn, and they concentrated their enquiries on finding those who were responsible.

Even when a case reaches the courts, a person should not be found guilty of a crime if he does not understand what it is that he has done. However, this is not an area where the issues are black and white. It is quite possible that someone may not know exactly what will be the consequences of his action, but he may nonetheless know that he should not do it. In such circumstances he may well be found guilty. If a serious crime is committed, there is always the possibility that the person who did it may be admitted to a psychiatric hospital. In some cases, these hospitals will not admit a particular patient, and he may have to go to a special hospital such as Rampton or Moss Side.

There are rules, issued to the police, the aim of which is to ensure that mentally handicapped people are not treated in the same way as others when they are detained and interrogated. The rules state that if it appears to a police officer that a person (whether a witness or a suspect) whom he intends to interview has a mental handicap which raises a doubt whether the person can understand the questions put to him, or which makes the person especially likely to be open to suggestion, the officer should take particular care in putting questions and accepting the reliability of answers. When the officer decides that the person is mentally handicapped, then the interview should only take place in the presence of his parent, or some other person, for example a social worker or the house-parent of the home where he lives.

In Robert Draper's case, the police had said that, although he seemed slow, he did not appear to them to be mentally handicapped, and they saw no reason to think that anyone else needed to be present at the interview. This was understandable, because Robert had learnt, over the years, to respond to strangers in a co-operative way. He often repeated the words that they said to him, nodded, and agreed with any suggestion put to him.

In many areas, mentally handicapped people carry with them a card which states that they are a member of a Gateway Club, or attend an Adult Training Centre. As the police are given full information about the Clubs and the Centres, problems can often be avoided. Some parents, though, dislike the idea that their child should carry with him a form of certificate which says, in effect, that he is mentally handicapped, and they react against the idea. It is of course entirely a matter of choice, but if a card or a certificate is carried, the risk of arrest and misunderstanding must be less.

SEXUAL OFFENCES

Parents of handicapped children are of course especially sensitive regarding sexual matters, as they affect their children. It is not at all unusual for a handicapped person to have the same sexual capacity and emotions as other people. Some, however, lack any understanding of what sexual behaviour involves. For this reason, sex education is very important for handicapped people, as has been more fully discussed in Chapter 2. We are here concerned, however, with the law, and we must deal with the very difficult problem of sexual offences that involve handicapped people. It is not at all likely that they will themselves commit a sexual offence, because of their handicap, but it is not impossible. If allegations of this kind are made against a mentally handicapped person, the rules mentioned above will apply, just as they do to other allegations of crime. It is important that legal advice be sought as early as possible, and also the assistance of the local and regional branches of national organisations who have a particular understanding of the handicap from which the accused person suffers. Often, the combined efforts of a solicitor and the representative of such an organisation can stop a prosecution, especially if arrangements are made to prevent the difficulty from occurring a second time.

Far more common, unfortunately, are sexual offences committed against handicapped people, especially those who are mentally handicapped and therefore vulnerable. The law is embodied in the Sexual Offences Act 1967, which states that it is unlawful for a man to have sexual intercourse with a woman whom he knows or suspects to be severely mentally handicapped. Note here the emphasis on 'severely'; in the case of mild mental handicap, not only will a girl be especially vulnerable, but sexual intercourse with her (after she has reached the age of 16) will not be an offence, unless it is proved that it took place without her consent, in which case it would amount to rape. Whether a woman or girl is severely mentally handicapped is a matter for a psychologist, a psychiatrist, or some other qualified person to say, and their evidence would be necessary to any prosecution. There are similar rules relating to homosexual behaviour.

Mr and Mrs East, as they became older, decided that the time had come for their daughter Betty to go into a residential home run by the Local Council. There were men and women in the home, and each resident had his or her own separate bedroom. Betty was slightly physically handicapped, as she could only see with very strong bi-focal lenses in her glasses. She was also severely mentally handicapped. It did not occur to Mr and Mrs East that their daughter might become involved in any sexual activity because she was not particularly attractive, and they assumed that the home would have arrangements for separating the men and women at night. In fact, there were no such arrangements. Some of the female residents were only mildly handicapped, which meant that the Sexual Offences Act 1967 did not apply to them. Mrs East heard one day that the staff were in the habit of advising women in the home to use the contraceptive pill. This news distressed her greatly, and although it was perfectly clear that Betty had not in fact been having sexual intercourse, she did have a boy friend in the home, and she quite often joined him in his room. He also visited her from time to time.

Mr and Mrs East immediately went to a solicitor. He advised them that if the staff in the home knew that a man (whether handicapped or not) was having sexual intercourse with a severely handicapped woman, then they should certainly take steps to prevent it from happening again. Not only might they be criticised in public (scandals of this sort are especially interesting to the newspapers), but they might also be prosecuted for allowing the criminal act to take place. In the event, Betty East was moved to another home where all the residents were women. The Local Council was very apprehensive of the possible publicity that Mrs East might create, and took immediate action to prevent this.

Sexual behaviour is always a most sensitive area. If two handicapped people, both of whom are over 18 years of age, decide to have some form of sexual contact with one another, including sexual intercourse, neither of them being severely mentally handicapped, then no crime is involved. Other issues arise, of course: if this happens in a residential home, decisions have to be made by the staff as to the attitude they are to take. Parents who know where their child is to go after leaving home should certainly make enquiries about the policy adopted in the home, especially if they are anxious that their son or daughter should not become sexually involved with other people. We are not assuming here that all parents feel this way; there are some who have no objection at all to sexual activity, and would in fact want to encourage it, as they believe it to be both natural and comforting. Others will react with horror to such ideas. Difficulties will arise in those places where the attitudes of the parents and of the persons responsible for the care of a handicapped person are different.

4 Services

It is absolutely vital that a handicapped person should take advantage of such services as are available in his area. It is just as important that his parents, if they are looking after him, should know what these services are, because the time will come when his contact with these services will govern decisions that are made about his future. There are still many parents who prefer not to have contact with social workers or other staff of the statutory services. They think, quite rightly, that no one can do as effective a job as they can, and that other people will never be able to care for their own child as they do.

This attitude is all right for so long as their handicapped child depends totally on them, but most parents who read this book are concerned about what is going to happen when they are too old to look after him, or have died. The truth is that his future, in the years ahead, is going to depend on what they do *today*. This applies to every aspect of his life, and certainly to the statutory and other services that he will need in the future.

So parents must find out what welfare and other services are available. By law, all Local Authorities must publish information about welfare services, and must ensure that anyone who uses one part of these services is told of any others that may be relevant to his needs. This law is contained in the Chronically Sick and Disabled Persons Act 1970, but no one will be surprised to learn that it is not always observed. However, parents working together can remind the Authorities of their legal obligations, and are entitled to be given details of the welfare services that are in fact provided in their area.

The same Act of Parliament makes it a duty for Local

Authorities to make and keep a note - usually known as a register - of the number of people who are blind, deaf or dumb, and others who are 'handicapped, substantially or permanently, by illness, injury, or congenital deformity, or such other disabilities as may be prescribed by the Minister.' Parents should visit the Local Authority to see if in fact they do have such a list, and to make sure that their own child's name is on it, even if he does not at present need any of the welfare services provided. If the Local Authority has not drawn up such a list, it is legally obliged to do so. Working together, parents can make sure that it does.

Another provision of the Chronically Sick and Disabled Persons Act 1970 (Section 2) is that a Local Authority must make arrangements for:

a   The provision of practical assistance for a person in his home.
b   The provision of, or assistance in obtaining, recreational facilities in his home.
c   The provision of, or assistance in obtaining, recreational facilities outside his home, and assistance in taking advantage of educational facilities.
d   The provision of facilities or assistance in travelling to and from the home to take part in welfare facilities.
e   Assistance in adapting the home for greater safety, comfort or convenience.
f   Facilitating the taking of holidays.
g   Provision of meals.
h   Provision of or assistance in obtaining a telephone or any special equipment necessary to enable him to use a telephone.

There are, of course, some handicapped people who can only take advantage of a few of these facilities, but the Local Authority has no choice in the matter: it must provide them. In practice, a good deal of pressure may be necessary to see that it does. For example, as part of the economy drives undertaken by many Councils in recent years, it is now found that the amount of money available to provide holidays for handicapped people has been severely cut back. In some areas it also takes a great deal of pressure on Authorities before they are willing to provide, or pay for, transport so that handicapped people can go to recreational clubs.

A statement was issued by the Independent Development Council for People with Mental Handicap, giving the principles on which a local service should be based. Such a service, it is stated, should value handicapped people as full citizens, with rights and responsibilities; they should be entitled to be consulted about their needs, and have a say in the plans being made to meet those needs, no matter how severe their handicap may appear to be at first sight. There are many forms of physical handicap that may, quite wrongly, give people the impression that the person suffering from them is also mentally handicapped. Spasticity is one of these. In fact, a very high proportion of spastic people are perfectly capable of explaining their needs, and so are many mentally handicapped people. One young man said recently:

'I'd like to learn how to read, so that people wouldn't laugh at me.'

He had never been taught, as no one had thought it worth while or even possible, but within a year he was already able to read simple stories, and it was not long before he found it easy to understand most items in the popular newspapers.

The Independent Development Council (IDC) went on to say that services should promote the independence and develop the skills and abilities of handicapped people and their families, and should design programmes of help that are based on the unique needs of each individual. They should also be helped to use the ordinary services and resources of the local community, e.g. primary care, education, health, social, employment, housing, welfare and recreational services. They want to see co-ordinated multi-disciplinary specialist services, delivered by appropriately trained staff. For mentally handicapped people, they recommend a Community Mental Handicap Team (CMHT) for each population unit of 60,000 people. A few such teams already exist: the core of the team is usually a community mental handicap nurse and a specialist social worker, but other specialists should be available, such as physiotherapists, speech therapists, teachers and psychologists. All services, the IDC states, should be easily accessible and given regardless of the handicapped person's age, or the severity of his disability. They should be made available at his home, or at his place of work, school or Adult Training Centre. Everything that the IDC says about the needs of mentally handicapped people is also true for those whose disability is physical, not mental.

Those are statements of the ideal services that ought to exist. If they are to be achieved in reality, it will be through the efforts of interested people, especially those who have a handicapped relative. If we look back thirty and more years, we can see considerable advances: since 1971, all people have become entitled to an education between the ages of five and eighteen, even if they suffer from severe handicap; plans are developing to bring all handicapped people out of hospital, unless it is necessary for them to stay there for medical care and treatment. The aim is that they should live in the community. Progress here will depend not only on the laws passed by Parliament, but on the efforts of parents, relatives and others who have a personal interest in progress, to bring pressure on the Authorities.

Let us therefore consider the way in which services for handicapped people have developed, and the manner in which they now operate. Over 650 years ago, a statute was passed entitled *De Praerogativa Regis* (1325). It showed a very clear understanding, on the part of people at that time, of the difference between people who were suffering from mental illness, and those who were mentally handicapped. It was well understood that a person who was mentally ill could some-times be cured, but that there was no cure for mental handicap.

Five hundred years after *De Praerogativa Regis*, our society began to segregate its poor, its handicapped and its old people into Poor Law Workhouses. An Act of Parliament was passed in 1834 to deal with those people who were regarded as 'lazy and shiftless'. Since that time, many men and women of low intelligence have been condemned to life in massive institutions, often built to keep them away from the rest of society. In these institutions the sexes were segregated, for it was believed that the law should ensure that those whom it regarded as 'unfit' should not be allowed 'to propagate their own kind'.

Under the Mental Deficiency Act 1913, 'idiots, imbeciles and feeble-minded persons' were classed with 'moral defectives', clear evidence of the extraordinary state of ignorance and prejudice that then existed. Handicapped people were depersonalised and stripped of their humanity. Even today there are still some women in mental handicap hospitals who are totally institutionalised, and whose only reason for being there is that they had an illegitimate baby many years ago, or were merely known to be promiscuous. Their punishment for this social crime has been to live in hospital for fifty years and more, often helping the staff with their work, but receiving no pay.

In some cases, the segregation of handicapped people from the rest of the community was based on other motives. In the Idiots Act 1886 there was a provision that 'care, education and training' should be provided for mentally handicapped people. This was often done by erecting specially designed buildings in the countryside. Inevitably, these buildings became institutions, not schools; as far as the rest of society was concerned, their residents were out of sight and out of mind.

The advent of intelligence tests in the early part of the twentieth century did not help. They tended to create the impression that mentally handicapped people were ineducable, which has since been proved to be entirely false. Not until 1971 were they given the right to attend school, and it was only by the Mental Health Act 1983 that those people who are mentally handicapped were again properly distinguished, by law, from those who are mentally ill. It will take many more years to eradicate prejudice against mentally handicapped people from the public mind, and to return to the more sensible and realistic attitudes that prevailed over 600 years ago.

The services now provided for handicapped people fall into these categories:

Assessment
Health
Education and Training
Welfare
Day Care
Residential Accommodation
Financial Support
Leisure and Recreation
Employment
Visiting Services

Parents should consider each service, and the way in which it can be of help to their child both today and in the future.

ASSESSMENT

It is not often apparent that a child is physically or mentally handicapped until he is two, three or even older. Some children become handicapped, through illness or an accident, while they are still young. Many parents have great difficulty in accepting the fact of handicap and are reluctant to have an assessment made, for fear of what it will show. This is absolutely natural, but of course the earlier a child's handicap is identified, the sooner it will be possible to obtain the right type of help, and training, for him. Assessment must always be linked to treatment, care and education.

There are Child Health Clinics with facilities for assessment and screening. Parents may be referred to them by the family doctor. The clinics help with feeding and health problems, and they should also be involved in any treatment that is given. The service given by the clinics can confuse parents, because they are working in parallel with the family doctor, and possibly also with the Health Visitor. Sometimes, they seem to work quite separately from other services in which case the parent has no alternative but to ask them to make contact, so that the advice she receives makes overall sense. In an ideal world, of course, there would be regular and effective communication between the various professionals who have seen her child, but it does not always work out this way. Professionals may be better at their own job than they are at liaison with other workers in the same field. In many cases, it is the parents themselves who have to act as a bridge.

In some areas, there are Multi-disciplinary Assessment Centres, where a child's intelligence, his body functions, his behaviour and his social and educational needs can be examined. Teachers, paediatricians, social workers, psychologists, therapists and others are all available to build up a picture of the handicap and of the best way of dealing with it. These centres are mostly in hospitals, because it is convenient to run them this way, and because it is to the family doctor that parents first turn when they begin to suspect that their child may be suffering from some kind of handicap.

Parents are of course entitled to an explanation of the results of the assessments made by clinics and by Assessment Centres, and will plan their child's future on the basis of the advice they are given. As soon as any physical problem is identified, it will be possible to take the process of assessment a stage further: Local Education Authorities have a duty, by law, to find out which children require special education, and then to make suitable provision for it, unless of course the parents themselves are able to afford alternative arrangements.

In most areas, handicapped children can now attend Nursery Schools from the age of two, and will go on to a Special School (or to the Special Education Section of an ordinary school) at age five. It is at this time that further regular assessment, through the keeping of records, is so important. Many Nurseries and Schools provide it; some do not. Parents, hoping for an improvement in their child's condition, should work together to ensure that the schools do in fact keep careful records of progress and have available the advice of experts, such as an educational psychologist, to help prepare a programme for each individual child. Work in many parts of the world has shown that, especially in the case of a handicapped child, an individual plan to suit his own needs and his level of understanding can help him to achieve a better life in the years to come.

On leaving school, also, handicapped people need to be assessed. It is very likely that they will be able to benefit from further education, and they will certainly be entitled to stay on at school until they reach nineteen. Whether they then transfer to an Adult Training Centre, a College of Further Education, an Industrial Training Unit or into open employment will depend on their known abilities and on their interests. Parents must see to it that the process of assessment of their child does not stop when the handicap is first diagnosed, but continues throughout his growing years.

HEALTH

As we have seen, there was a time when most matters relating to handicapped people were the responsibility of doctors, and later of the Health Service. It then came to be recognised that handicapped people had many needs which the medical profession was not equipped to provide. Nevertheless, a handicapped person does have health needs, and may well be more prone to sickness than others. He may require special aids to help him walk, to go to the toilet, and to hear and see.

Each handicapped person will have a family doctor. The doctor will probably have a Health Visitor attached to his practice, whose job is to see all children under the age of five, either at home or at a Health Clinic. There are also Physiotherapists, Speech Therapists, Home Nurses and Home Helps who may be able to help. The best way to obtain these services is to ask the family doctor to make arrangements for them to be provided; they may also be organised through the Health Clinic. It is of course easier for families in and around the towns and cities to obtain this type of help than it is for those living in the country where a return journey to an Assessment Centre or a Health Clinic can take a whole day.

No one relishes a visit to the dentist, and many handicapped people find it particularly trying. Like others, however, if they are able to develop a relationship of trust with the dentist, they can cope with the pain they may have to endure, especially now that pain-killing injections are given. A visit to the optician is much less alarming, but it is equally important that the handicapped patient, even while quite young, should become used to such visits and learn that dentists, opticians and others exist to help, are friendly, and can be trusted. Parents should not surround the visit with mystery or anxiety, but should explain what is going on and what will happen. Confidence established at an early age, especially by the child who is physically handicapped and may over the years have to face extended treatment, including operations, will help him to cope with worry, pain, and even with loneliness.

EDUCATION AND TRAINING

No child is now considered to be outside the education system. All children who need special educational provision are entitled to it. They will attend an ordinary school, if practicable; otherwise they will go to a Special School. The Education Authority is under a legal duty to ensure that the parents of a handicapped child are involved in assessments of their children, and kept fully informed. It must make an assessment if the parents require it, six months after the previous assessment, as long as the request is reasonable. A child under the age of two must be assessed if his parents so desire.

Until 1970, the education of handicapped children was the responsibility of the Health Authorities, many of whom decided that a particular child was 'ineducable'. From 1971, the Education Authorities were given the task of education, under the terms of the Education (Handicapped Children) Act 1970. Under the Education Act 1944 all children, including those who are handicapped, are now entitled to education from age five until they attain their nineteenth birthday. Because of their condition, many mentally handicapped people need education over a long period; it may take them years to learn what others can be taught in a much shorter time. Parents should under no circumstances accept a statement by a school head, or by an Education Authority, that their child can no longer benefit from education after reaching the age of sixteen. If necessary, they should obtain legal advice to ensure that their child continues at school. There is a note on the appropriate legislation in Appendix II. When threatened with legal action, more than one Local Authority has changed its mind and allowed a particular handicapped child to stay at school for an extra two years. There are, of course, many enlightened Authorities who encourage this, and who recognise that a handicapped person has the same right to further education, after attaining the age of nineteen, as anyone else.

When making assessments, Local Education Authorities must first inform the parents, and must take account of anything that they wish to say (Education Act 1981). They may make a statement of the child's needs, and if they do this they must send a copy to the parents who then have a chance to make comments. The statement must be renewed at least once a year, and there must be a special assessment between the ages of twelve years six months and thirteen years six months. There are Special Schools, divided between ESN (S), which stands for 'Educationally Sub-Normal: Severe', and ESN (M), meaning 'Educationally Sub-Normal: Mild'.

Obviously it is of the greatest importance for a handicapped child to go to the right school and to receive an education matched to his abilities, as well as his disabilities. The parent who is concerned about what will happen in the more distant future should take as much care in placing his handicapped child in the most suitable school as he does with non-handicapped children, if not more. This may involve a demand for an assessment and visits to the Education Authority.

Understandably, many parents feel diffident about making demands of this kind, and about questioning the decisions of a Statutory Authority; but if they are uncertain, or believe that the wrong decision has been made about their child's future, they must stick to their guns. Help is available, not only from the legal profession, but from the representatives of voluntary organisations. See the list of names and addresses given in Appendix IV.

Beyond education there is training. There is no doubt at all that many handicapped people can be trained for work. The organisation Remploy is exclusively concerned with this, and there are other organisations, e.g. Mencap's Pathway Scheme, described later in this chapter, which provide work for those who are handicapped. Throughout the country there are Adult Training Centres, so named because it was originally intended that they would prepare handicapped people for work in the community. At that time, there were more jobs available than there are today. Unfortunately, there has been a tendency for many of the Centres to provide only some simple occupation, rather than training. Some have taken on 'contract work' from manufacturers, which makes little or no demands on the 'trainees' who fit small plastic items together, or pack goods into envelopes. The Centres, and the Local Authorities who run them, make a fair income from this contract work, while the handicapped people are often paid little or nothing for what they do.

Some fortunate handicapped people are given real training, so that they can later find industrial, agricultural or horticultural work. Also, there are some Adult Training Centres which have set up self-sufficient businesses of their own, and can pay a reasonable wage to the people who work there. In addition, there are sheltered workshops where employees, having received proper training, are able to carry on a satisfying job, with professional supervision and a reasonable salary.

Perhaps the most valuable form of preparation for life in the community is social training. Living at home, many handicapped people are so well protected that they are not used to managing for themselves. Washing and keeping a room tidy, laundering clothes and cooking simple meals are skills that some of them are never given the chance to develop. Ideally, every handicapped person should begin to learn these skills at home, but where this is not practicable, or has simply not happened, it may well be that he or she can be taught such skills at school, at an Adult Training Centre, or at a Local Authority Hostel. Several Centres and Hostels have special units where trainees and residents can be trained to manage for themselves; as a result, many of them are able to cope more effectively at home, and some go on to live in group homes or other accommodation where, with supervision, they have a secure future.

WELFARE

Welfare services for the families of handicapped people are generally provided by the Social Services Departments of Local Authorities, but many are supplemented by the work of voluntary organisations. In fact, following the running-down of many Social Services Departments in recent years, as a result of the economic recession, social workers are often only able to provide an emergency service at best, and little supportive casework.

Under the Chronically Sick and Disabled Persons Act 1970, Local Authority Social Services Departments are put under a duty to provide residential care, fostering, day nurseries and support in the home. It is supposed to be the task of the social workers to discover the need and then to arrange for these, and other, services to be provided. In fact, social workers are frequently too busy to help anyone who is not facing a crisis; they often do not have time to find out what services are available in the area; and some of them are at loggerheads with other statutory workers, for example Health Visitors and pre-school teachers. A parent may well receive a visit from these workers, each apparently unaware of the work of the others.

Parents who live in an area where there is close co-operation between the Social Services, Health, Education and Housing Authorities are more fortunate. Others have first to learn what officials there are and what they do, then to seek them out, discover what community resources exist to help their child, and see that they are actually made available. It is small wonder that many parents have banded together to share information with one another and to bring their combined pressure to bear upon the Authorities. Often, the parents themselves, and their representatives in voluntary organisations, are as well or better informed than the statutory officials themselves. Many officials remain only a short time in a particular job (promotion only being achieved by moving out of the district, or to another department).

Another problem is that a social worker, Health Visitor or other official will often be expected to carry responsibility for many clients in addition to those who are handicapped. Crises affecting old people and those who are homeless may have to come first, because they are immediate and urgent. The handicapped person may be able to wait for a day or two, or a week – and so he does.

These are some of the social services that a handicapped person may need, and that will probably be available:

Fostering care, short-term or long-term
Adoption
Home help
Training for parents
Toy libraries
Physical aids
Local recreation activities
Holidays
Short-term care (sometimes known as 'Respite care')

Parents may need to be persistent in finding out where and how these services can be delivered. Unfortunately, the search for this type of help can be long and discouraging. If a particular service simply does not exist in your area, then again it may be necessary to put pressure on the Social Services Department, drawing attention to the provisions of the Chronically Sick and Disabled Persons Act 1970, or other legislation that applies. Working together, families can achieve more than if they operate on their own, especially if they publicise their efforts and go direct to the elected councillors as well as to the officials of the Council. There are many cases where parents who have not succeeded in spurring a particular Local Authority into action have themselves set up self-help groups, for example mother-and-baby groups, toy libraries and training schemes.

Many voluntary organisations are good at making this type of provision, and at bringing political pressure. Grants may be available for voluntary schemes which the Local Council is not itself prepared to carry out, but may be willing to support. There are sometimes officials of Local Authorities who would very much like to see a new or improved service, but who cannot speak out in favour of it because of their official position. There is nothing to prevent parents from doing so, individually, in groups, or through the representatives of their national organisation. In many areas, the regional staff of voluntary organisations have been able to persuade Local Authorities to provide a new service, where they are legally empowered to do so. The officials and Councillors often know very little about the problems of mental handicap. It is necessary to educate them, by bringing them face-to-face with the people concerned, and with their families. Once this has been done they are more aware that the needs of handicapped people require just as much attention as those of the old and the homeless.

It is all too easy for parents to give up the struggle to identify or establish the services that they want to see, and instead to provide them all themselves. By doing this, they ensure that their child is well cared for, but only for so long as they remain in good health. If they take no action until they face old age, it will probably be too late for them to affect their child's future. It is at this point that their anxieties will begin to grow and, having spent most of their lives caring for their handicapped child, they face the future with growing despair. There is only one answer - at least until the day comes when the State can and does make full provision for all who need help: parents must themselves take steps to see that services are created. They must do this while they are still strong and determined enough to achieve it.

DAY CARE

The aim of Day Care services is to provide care and education for mentally handicapped people, and support for their families. Day Nurseries and Special Schools have already been mentioned, but Social Services Departments sometimes also offer Playgroups for children in the age range two to five. Playgroups vary: some give a simple opportunity for handicapped children to play with toys and with one another, and also aim to help them develop simple skills; others - often known as 'Opportunity Groups' - have specially designed stimulation programmes, with sessions devised by therapists and psychologists. These Playgroups can lift a great burden from parents and can enable their children to develop social and other skills. Local Authorities have the power to provide them, but are not legally obliged to do so. Again, therefore, parents should seek out the groups, if they exist; if they do not, then pressure may have to be put on the Local Authority to provide them.

After leaving school, the majority of handicapped people are likely to go to an Adult Training Centre, or possibly to a sheltered workshop. Most of the Centres were built in the 1960s and 1970s, and the service they provide varies considerably. Some aim to train handicapped people to find a job in open employment; some only provide repetitive work from which the handicapped people (usually known as 'trainees') learn little or nothing. A survey found that only a little more than a quarter of the staff at Adult Training Centres had any relevant qualification, and that many of the 'trainees' were in fact employed on 'contract work'. One can visit Centres today where handicapped people are doing only the simplest of tasks. While the Centre itself (on behalf of the Local Authority Social Services Department) negotiates a commercial rate for the job, the trainees are often only paid a very small sum each week, calculated at a level which will avoid their loss of any State Benefits.

Mr and Mrs Harries felt that their son Philip was achieving nothing at the Adult Training Centre which he attended. With proper training, they thought, he could certainly manage to do work that was both useful and interesting, but his day consisted of putting together the pieces of cheap plastic toys. His mother and father complained to the manager of the Centre, who replied: 'Well, you can take him away, if you like. There are lots of others who'll be glad to have his place.'

It is threats of this kind that cause many parents to stifle their criticisms of Training Centres, homes and even hospitals. Mr and Mrs Harries decided to go straight to the Director of Social Services for the county, and to enlist the help of several other parents. The manager of the Centre was fortunately due for retirement in a short time; he had been appointed after some years' work as a factory manager and saw his job as a way of keeping handicapped people occupied rather than trained. He also had been given instructions to find contract work, so as to reduce the cost of running the Centre. The result was an activity which had no particular purpose other than to keep the 'trainees' occupied. After a time, he was replaced by a manager with relevant qualifications and new ideas. The contract work was given up and the Centre began a varied programme involving the manufacture of garden furniture and wrought-iron work, and other activities. Trainees were moved from one task to another, and some were able to find open employment because of the skills they had learnt.

One problem faced by Adult Training Centres is that the results they produce depend to a large extent on the work of the most skilled trainees. The result is that a manager whose Centre is doing good work likes to retain the best people in the jobs they are doing and does not want to lose them. Thus the aim of the Centres can be defeated. The 'star pupils' are kept at the Centre, to make sure that its standards are maintained. It is quite clear, however, that most parents are glad that their handicapped children have something to do each day; the constant burden of care is lifted from their shoulders for five days each week.

After a large number of Centres were built during the 1960s and 1970s, the rate slowed down, and waiting lists are now beginning to build up. There are areas in which young handicapped people leaving school have nowhere to go, causing great worry and anger on the part of parents who have become used to their child being out of the house all day during term time. This has led to some older trainees being 'retired' from Centres when they reach the age of fifty, or younger. A bleak prospect faces them at this time, and it often coincides with the period when their parents - or their surviving parent - can no longer cope with them at home.

Parents of children still at a Special School should make early plans for the transfer of their child to a Centre at the time when he is likely to complete his education, unless of course they want him to pursue some other kind of activity, for example in a sheltered workshop. Unfortunately, this is an option which is not often available: it has been found that it is eleven times more difficult to find a place in a sheltered workshop than in open employment, which in itself is no easy task. Progress in the development of new Adult Training Centres and workshops is very slow, because little money is available for capital building projects. Only by working together in large numbers can parents expect to bring significant pressure on Local Authorities to put Day Care facilities for handicapped people at the top of their list of priorities.

RESIDENTIAL ACCOMMODATION

Local Authorities were obliged under the National Assistance Act 1948 to provide accommodation of various types, suited to the needs of people who had no home of their own. This covered a very large number of people, and as national resources decreased during the 1970s it became necessary to establish some priorities. By the Housing (Homeless Persons) Act 1977, priority groups were named. Those who are physically or mentally handicapped and are homeless or threatened with homelessness are given such priority, and the Local Authorities must make provision for them. It is also Government policy to discharge from the mental handicap hospitals all those people who need not be there, as they are not in need of medical treatment, but only supervision and care. The aim is that they should be housed in the community, and this will result in a major transfer of resources from the Health Service to Local Authorities. There is a detailed note on the legislation in Appendix II.

The conditions in some mental handicap hospitals are good. In many, there are caring staff doing their best to cope with large numbers of patients. Because of understaffing, the time they are able to give to each handicapped person is all too limited, but they do their best. From time to time, scandals break in the press and on television, exposing poor conditions and even – though very occasionally – cruelty. The buildings in which the patients live and the staff work were mostly erected over one hundred years ago, at a time when the attitude of society was that it was best to place handicapped people out of contact with the rest of the community.

Government policy has changed, but money resources remain scarce. Transfer of patients from hospitals to homes is slow. Staff in the Health Service may be worried about the security of their jobs, and this does nothing to increase the pace of transfer. Mental handicap hospitals will be with us for many years to come, and while the service provided in some is excellent, accommodation standards leave much to be desired. Plans for the future are for hospital units with hundreds rather than thousands of beds, but money is short and progress is not likely to be quick. There is some prospect of change, if only because it costs more to keep a patient in hospital for a year than it does in a home or a hostel. In some parts of the country, for example in Wessex, it has been proved that the Health Service can run small houses, in the community, for severely handicapped people, fully staffed and supported by all necessary medical services.

Residential provision by Local Authorities falls into these main categories:

Hostels
Group homes
Fostering
Boarding out

Most Local Authority *hostels* are in converted houses or in specially designed buildings. There are normally communal eating and washing facilities for residents, with one or more lounges for relaxation. Residents often have a room of their own, but some are expected to share a room and are quite content with this arrangement. Most hostels have four or more senior staff members, some of whom have qualifications in child care or in subnormality nursing. The majority of handicapped people who have lived both in hospital and in a hostel say that they prefer the latter, even though some hostels tend to become institutional in character.

Group homes established by Local Authorities are usually provided for those handicapped people who need very little supervision or support. Residents naturally tend to be people who have relatively mild forms of handicap. Places in group homes are often allocated to former residents of hostels who have already shown themselves able to cope particularly well. Some group homes have resident wardens or house-parents, and in some there are handicapped people living with others, for example students, who are not handicapped. The support of visiting social workers and other professionals is normally available.

Parents tend to prefer the maximum levels of supervision

and support for their children. Having provided constant care for many years, they find it difficult to believe that their child can live a relatively independent life, after being given a period of training. In fact, it is the experience of most professionals working in the field that a great many of those with handicap can, given encouragement, manage to do more than their parents have allowed them to attempt.

Some parents are glad to take advantage of the *fostering* schemes that have become established in areas such as Somerset and Leeds, where families with grown or growing children are willing to take a handicapped person into their home on a permanent or semi-permanent basis.

There has always been a number of Local Authorities who, in exercising their legal responsibilities, have placed handicapped people in *boarding houses*, or small hotels. These are privately run homes, the owners of which are making their living by providing for a limited number of handicapped residents. Experience shows that this can be a very profitable enterprise, and it has been taken up by a large number of Local Authorities who find that it is still cheaper from their point of view than building, maintaining and staffing a hostel or a group home. There is obviously the risk that some people will set up boarding houses with the sole intention of making money, and without much interest in the welfare of handicapped people. Some examples of this have already occurred, but the Health and Social Services and Social Security Adjudications Act 1983 has made provision for the inspection of all such houses, using guidelines issued by the Department of Health and Social Security.

Bearing in mind the facilities that exist, what is actually happening? When the parents of a handicapped child die, or become too old to care for him, where does he go and who cares for him?

Much depends on the steps that his parents and relatives have already taken to provide for his future. For example, the

SERVICES 83

couple who have arranged for their handicapped child to spend
occasional weekends and holiday periods at a nearby hostel may
be able to obtain an assurance from the Local Authority that
their child will be able to live there, when the time comes.

Unfortunately, for a disturbingly large number of handicapped people, the fact is that, when they are left on their own,
everything depends on the immediate action taken, whether by
a social worker, a family doctor, the police or some other
person. Often, the Health and the Social Services Authorities
try to shift the immediate responsibility for care from one to
another. Great pressure may be put on members of the
handicapped person's family to solve the problem by taking
him into their own home. Once there, the Authorities often
show no willingness to accept him in a hospital, hostel or group
home. As one distinguished professional has said: 'They lie
where they fall.'

Some examples can be given, each based on cases that
occurred during the year before the publication of this book, of
what may happen.

Case A   A mother had two children, a girl aged 16 and a
handicapped boy of 14. Her husband was an alcoholic. She
developed cancer and died. The father was not interested in
his son's future, and a social worker managed to obtain a
place for the boy in a hostel in a large city several miles away
from his home. He lived there for a while, but began to come
home occasionally for weekends. On one such visit his 16
year-old sister was very distressed to find that he was ill,
suffering from influenza, and that no one had made any
attempt to find him treatment. She kept him at home for a
while and decided that it would be wrong for him to go back
to the hostel which appeared to care so little for him. She
contacted the social worker who said, 'Don't bother me - I
got him into the hostel, didn't I?' Eventually, a voluntary
organisation found a small flat for the girl and her brother,
where they now live.

Case B   A woman took her mother and her handicapped sister into her own home when the mother fell ill. The mother died, and the woman was told by a social worker that she would have to continue to look after her handicapped sister indefinitely. She protested that she could not do this, but no action was taken to help her, or to provide accommodation for her sister. After some time, she managed to obtain short-term care for her handicapped sister, on a regular weekend basis. One day, after the sister had spent a few days in the short-term unit, the woman refused to take her back.

Case C   The sole surviving parent of a 42 year-old handicapped man died suddenly one day while he was at an Adult Training Centre. The manager of the ATC telephoned his superior at the Social Services Department, and the man was taken to a hospital which declined to take any responsibility for him. He was placed that night in a geriatric home where the residents were for the most part twice his age, many of them senile. He is still there.

Case D   A charity opened a home for mentally handicapped people, encouraged by the local Social Services Department. A lot of money was raised in the neighbourhood to build, equip and furnish the house. Residents were selected from families where parents were very old, and also from a local hospital. A few weeks before it was due to be opened by a national celebrity, the organisers of the home were told that the Social Services Department could not afford the money to sponsor any residents; the home remained half-full. One handicapped man who could and should have gone there was placed in a psychiatric hospital which was entirely unsuitable to his condition.

Case E   A residential school, also run by a charity, was caring for an orphaned girl until she reached the age of 19, after which the Local Education Authority which had sponsored her refused to continue to pay the fees. The Health and Social Services Authorities in the area from which she had originally come declined to take any responsibility for her. Ultimately, the School Head took the girl to a nearby mental handicap hospital and left her there. Some years later, she was still there, although there was no indication that she required medical treatment.

Case F A charity ran a residential community for handicapped people. A woman was accepted there, sponsored by a Local Authority and also by a modest contribution made by her aged parents. After some time she began to behave in a way the charity did not like. They refused to keep her there, and her parents took her home before trying to persuade the Local Authority to take her into one of their homes. The Authority refused to do this because, they said, they had no room for her. The parents were left in despair as to what would happen when they could no longer manage to cope with their daughter, whose behaviour was increasingly difficult.

Case G In the area of one Local Authority, handicapped people whose parents have died are first placed in a large hospital. If they do not require medical treatment they are then moved to short-term hostel accommodation, if any places are available. If there are no places, the handicapped men and women are 'boarded-out' in privately-run homes. In one such home the residents are instructed to leave the building by 9.15 am. They are allowed back for lunch and must then go out again, whatever the weather, until 5.30 pm. From the fees charged by the owner of the boarding house, and the level of staffing there, it would seem that he is making a very considerable profit out of the operation.

FINANCIAL SUPPORT

There is a wide variety of financial provision for handicapped people and their families, by way of benefits, pensions and allowances. It is very important that all these benefits should be claimed, but the rules and regulations governing them are complex. The provisions were explained in Chapter 3, but anyone in doubt should seek advice. (See Chapter 5.)

LEISURE AND RECREATION

Handicapped people benefit as much from a holiday and from recreation as anyone else. Local Authorities must give financial help to enable them to take part in recreational activities, and to have holidays. See the reference to the Chronically Sick and Disabled Persons Act 1970 at the beginning of this chapter. Money for this purpose can also be provided by the *Family Fund*, a Government scheme administered by the Joseph Rowntree Memorial Trust. Various local and national voluntary organisations, including Mencap, run holidays each year, using professional staff and volunteer workers. Mencap also publishes a Guide to Holiday Accommodation and has a national network of about 600 leisure clubs, operating under the name 'Gateway'. These clubs provide opportunities for mentally handicapped people to meet each other, and to play games and sports. There are regional, national and international competitions and festivals, organised largely with the help of volunteers. Many other organisations also organise sporting and social events for people with widely differing handicaps. Whenever possible, the parents of handicapped children should try to ensure that they take part in leisure activities and holidays. Not only do these provide stimulation and amusement, but they help the handicapped children to relate to one another, and to enjoy a wide range of new experiences. Parents are almost always surprised at the extent of their children's achievements.

EMPLOYMENT

At a time of high national unemployment, men and women with physical or mental handicap face enormous difficulties in finding a job. In all parts of the country, Disablement Resettlement Officers (DROs) exist, attached to Local Authorities. The facilities at their disposal include Remploy Workshops where handicapped people carry on a variety of activities and are paid at least the minimum wage for the job. Many firms are willing to employ a fixed proportion of physically handicapped people in suitable work. The DROs tend to spend the greater part of their time trying to place physically handicapped people, because of the existence of the Adult Training Centres which, for the most part, help those who are mentally handicapped. It is a fact, however, that only a small proportion of handicapped people can expect to find employment.

Mencap runs an employment scheme called 'Pathway'. Financed almost entirely by Local Authorities, often with the help of Urban Aid or Joint Funding Grants, Pathway appoints an officer whose task is to explain to employers the type of work that mentally handicapped people can do, and to ensure that they are given appropriate training for the specific job that is to be offered to them.

Many employers have found that staff who have reached them by way of the Pathway Service are reliable, conscientious and good time-keepers. The Pathway Officer identifies some other person in the shop or factory, who acts as a friend to the handicapped employee and helps to solve any small problems he may encounter. Having taken on mentally handicapped people with some reservations, many employers have returned to the Pathway Service with a request for more workers.

The Pathway Officers do face one problem when discussing possible employment with the parents of some young mentally handicapped people: parents are often doubtful whether their son or daughter could or should do the type of work that has been offered. Problems are also encountered when a crisis occurs at work; many Pathway Officers have been called out during the evening after a telephone call from parents who report: 'Peter says he's not going back to work tomorrow morning.' The problems can usually be dealt with quite simply, but an essential role of the Pathway Officer is to continue to keep an eye on the people whom he has succeeded in placing in a job. There have even been cases where parents have been reluctant to allow their child to go out to work, because it may involve a reduction in the benefits received. In one case, these benefits amounted to about £3 a week more than the salary that would be paid, and the young man who had found a job was prevented from taking it by his family. Such action, though understandable, is short-sighted, for the experience of working in open employment is of very great value to a handicapped person, and stands him in good stead in future years.

VISITING SERVICES

Many charities, Hospital Friends Groups and other voluntary organisations make arrangements for a handicapped person who lives in a hospital, a hostel or a group home to be befriended and visited by someone who is willing to take a permanent interest in his welfare. There is at least one major hospital where the Friends Group has organised a large number of volunteers so that every patient receives a regular visit.

Mencap operates a visitors service, known as the 'Trustee Visitors Service' because it operates under the terms of a Trust Deed. Parents, relations and others are invited to make a contribution (£2,500 at the time of publication) to Mencap, and they nominate a particular individual whom they wish to benefit from the service. Because of the provisions of Charity and Tax Law, no binding contract can be entered into to visit a particular person, but in fact it is normally possible to provide visitors not only to those who have been nominated, but also to others. The service operates when the parents of the 'beneficiary' have died; a visitor normally sees the beneficiary once a month, and gives small presents and cards at Christmas and on birthdays. Visitors also give a regular report to Mencap about the health and the circumstances of the handicapped beneficiary, and if any problem arises a member of Mencap's staff is available to approach the hospital, hostel or home in an attempt to resolve the difficulty.

From what has necessarily been a brief summary it can be seen that there is a great range of services, both statutory and voluntary, available to help handicapped people. Parents should check carefully through this chapter in order to ensure that they have considered all the possibilities. The help and support they obtain today will not only lighten their own burden; it may improve the life of their handicapped child in the present and the future. Parents and relatives who are uncertain about the availability of services in their own area should obtain advice. The best way to do this is discussed in the following chapter.

5 Advice

Advice can be obtained on every aspect of handicap: medical, legal, social, educational and financial. Although there is a lot of advice in this book, no book can answer questions; nor can it deal with the precise circumstances of every handicapped person and his family. Yet competent advice is essential, if a sensible plan for the future of a handicapped person is to be developed.

As we have seen, parents are entitled to an assessment of their child's handicap. This should be obtained, and reviewed regularly, because it is on the basis of assessments that advice will be given on the way in which a handicapped child can best be educated and trained. The problem, of course, is to get the right advice from the right person. Which is the right doctor, the best teacher, the most effective therapist? On whom can one rely for advice on the best social life for one's child after he leaves school? Who is best placed to judge when, if at all, he should leave home and go to live with others of his own age? Which solicitor can one approach? How can one be sure that he really does know the law that will apply to one's child?

Often, we think that we are more likely to be right than the professionals. How many parents have rejected the advice of a doctor, or of a social worker, which they feel may lead their child into a situation of risk? How many have become determined to protect their child from the pressures of the outside world, and are only willing to accept advice that fits in with this determination?

One great difficulty is that advice is available from a very large number of people with no professional qualifications at all, who are very willing to say: 'If I were you . . .' Unfortunately, they are often passing on their own misunderstandings of medicine or the law, and making the assumption that schemes which have worked for them will automatically suit everyone else. What is more, people like to reassure themselves that the decisions they have taken are right, so they pass on these decisions - in the form of advice - to other people.

It is difficult enough that there are many people who like to pass on their own experience in this way. To make matters worse, many professionals lack the skill and knowledge to give accurate advice to the families of handicapped people. Unfortunately, it is only too easy to obtain poor advice, and misinformation.

Mr Black had no idea what provision he should make in his will for his mentally handicapped daughter Joan. He had heard that there would be a lot of complications if he simply left her a share of his property, but he still wanted to make some arrangement which would provide her with extra comforts, over and above what the State would give. He talked to the father of another handicapped girl, who assured him that the answer was perfectly simple: he should set up a discretionary trust for her in his will, and all would be well. This was what the second man had done, on the advice of his solicitor given some ten years previously.

Given the circumstances of Mr Black and his daughter Joan, this advice was nonsense, but unfortunately he decided his friend must be right, and changed his will to create a discretionary trust. He died a few years later, the owner of a large and valuable house. The house was sold, for Joan could not possibly live there on her own, and because of the regulations which allow Local Authorities to levy charges for residential accommodation (which they gave Joan), his daughter received no more benefit than if he had left her only a small sum.

What advice should Mr Black have been given? In the first place, neither he nor his friend knew that the new regulations had been brought into effect quite recently. These are described in later chapters, and some solutions are offered to the problem that faced Mr Black. The solicitor who made the friend's will was quite right at the time, but the law had changed. Mr Black's solicitor was unfortunately not aware of the new regulations (they had been brought into effect within a month of Mr Black's will being made), and the result was that the Local Authority took the major benefit under the will.

Good and accurate advice will be given by a professional person who has a thorough understanding of handicap, and practical experience to add to his existing technical knowledge. How are such people to be found? In Appendix IV are given the names and addresses of various organisations whose task it is to give practical advice and help, and who will be able to answer parents' questions. Many of them have lists of professional people to whom they regularly make referrals. Parents who are uncertain whether their own professional adviser is aware of the special factors that affect a handicapped person can obtain information, in the form of leaflets and pamphlets, from these organisations. This information they can then take to their legal, medical, educational or financial adviser.

In addition, there are in most areas groups of parents whose children suffer from the same form of handicap; these groups can often identify a professional person who has made a full study of the subject, and they refer parents to him. There is no professional difficulty here, because the person to whom the referrals have been made is not 'advertising' his services; on the contrary, people are coming to him because of the extra skills he possesses and the reputation he enjoys. This is how most professional people build up their practices.

The professional person on whom all parents will at some stage rely is their family doctor. In each medical practice there is always a number of handicapped people, but if a doctor is uncertain about the best way to help a patient, he will refer him to a consultant, or to a special clinic. Often this is the best answer, because no doctor can be expected to be familiar with the whole range of problems that can affect a handicapped person. Parents will of course give their doctor as much information as possible about their child; this he will put in his notes, which in turn will be seen by the specialists to whom he refers the child. In some areas, these specialists will form a group, for example a Community Mental Handicap Team, who can deal with the various needs of the handicapped person.

Professional advice on the education potential of a handicapped person will normally be obtained through the Local Education Authority, following an assessment which is obligatory under the Education Act 1981. As has already been noted, the Authorities must involve parents in the process of assessment. If a parent is not satisfied with an assessment, he can ask for another after a short period of time. Alternatively, if he can afford it, he may decide to go for a private assessment of his child. The organisations whose names and addresses are set out in Appendix IV will be able to give names of professionals who can help.

There is still a limited number of Local Education Authorities who try to discharge handicapped children from school at the age of sixteen, on the grounds that they 'cannot benefit from further education.' This is most unlikely to be the case, as it has been found that almost all people, whatever their handicap, can receive a benefit from education. Under these circumstances, parents can demand an assessment which will be made by a professionally qualified person. If dissatisfied with this assessment, it is open to them to seek independent advice, possibly from an educational psychologist.

Advice is often needed on State Benefits. The excellent *Disability Rights Handbook*, published by the Disability Alliance, will give valuable help. Most Local Authorities have appointed a Welfare Rights Officer, whose task it is to give advice on the entitlement to benefits of old and disabled people. It is very often in the interests of the Council to make this advice available, because those people who are not claiming all their State benefits may become a burden on the ratepayer. A Welfare Rights Officer will not normally give much help in regard to the services provided (or not provided) by the Local Council, because he is one of its employees. He is bound by its policy decisions. He is not likely, for example, to bring pressure on his own employer to change its policies on the provision of facilities for handicapped people.

Advice on welfare and rights may also be obtained from a Citizens' Advice Bureau, and possibly also from a Neighbourhood Law Centre. The regional offices of the organisations mentioned in the Appendix may also be able to help. There are solicitors available to advise at Citizens' Advice Bureaux, usually on a fixed evening each week. The Bureaux are in towns throughout the country, and can be found through the telephone book. The Neighbourhood Law Centres operate under various titles, and are usually supported by the Local Authority. Their main concern is with welfare matters, and with employment and tenancy problems. They can often help the parents of a handicapped child, but they do not normally do property work, nor make wills for clients. The Centres usually employ at least one solicitor, who directs the office and takes responsibility for the advice given there. Many Neighbourhood Law Centres are in small shops on street corners, with large notices drawing attention to the services they offer.

The notices at solicitors' offices are more modest. The firm's name may be painted on the windows in gold lettering, and there will be a plate near the door giving the name of the firm, often with the words 'Solicitors: Commissioners for Oaths' underneath. Most firms undertake legal aid work, and this fact is shown by the logo which they display in their window, showing two people seated at a table, facing one another. Few solicitors have a wide experience of welfare law, so it is important to go to the right firm. They are far more likely to deal with property, wills and company matters, but if questions of property affecting handicapped people are to be discussed, they will need to be familiar with the regulations affecting Supplementary Benefits and Local Authority Part III accommodation, explained in detail in Chapter 6. Parents who are members of a local Mencap society will probably be able to obtain the name of a firm which already has experience of these regulations. Alternatively, the regional staff of Mencap have a list of suitable solicitors.

It is very important to remember that the great majority of physically and mentally handicapped people will be entitled to Legal Aid and Advice. Having reached the age of 16, they can claim Supplementary Benefit. Anyone receiving this benefit is entitled, under the Legal Aid and Advice Scheme, to be given advice, and if necessary supported in making an application to a court. No contribution towards the cost of this service will have to be made, unless a large sum of money is recovered in an action for damages, in which case some part of the costs will have to be repaid to the Legal Aid Fund.

Many parents are worried that it is they who will have to pay a solicitor's bill, but if their handicapped child qualifies for legal advice under the Legal Aid and Advice Scheme, then they will not have to do so. What is more, legal advice under the scheme does not have to concern matters which may end in court; it is available, for example, on welfare matters and benefit claims.

There is a very natural temptation to 'do it yourself' when it comes to legal matters. Some people think that they can make their own wills, deal with property matters or handle disputes with the Authorities, on their own. So they can; but they often get it wrong, and leave themselves worse off as a result. It really does not make sense, when the future of a handicapped person is concerned, to take action without qualified legal advice. Naturally, this applies equally in the medical, educational and social fields as well as in the law. The well-meaning help of friends and relations who think that they have the answer to a problem, is no substitute for advice from someone who is properly qualified.

Mr and Mrs Potter had a 40 year-old son, Jack. He was mentally handicapped and had become very much overweight. Because of this, he moved around as little as he could, much preferring to sit in a chair and watch television. People who knew Jack said that a programme of exercise would help him to do more for himself, and also reduce his weight. His parents received professional advice that Jack could be given training for a wide variety of tasks, and that if he could be encouraged to move from his chair he would learn to dress himself, keep clean, and probably be able to prepare simple meals. His parents reacted against the whole idea. In the first place, they saw the suggested education programme for Jack as a kind of criticism of themselves, even though their doctor assured them that it would do Jack a lot of good to reduce his weight and take walks in the local park. Some time later, Jack's mother became ill and died in hospital. His father found it increasingly difficult to look after Jack, and asked the Council if they could find room for him in a nearby home that had just been built. Jack was one of those whose names were considered for admission to the home. The Council's selection committee considered his skills and his physical condition, and matched these against the skills and fitness of other would-be residents. Sadly, the fact that Jack was so overweight and could do little for himself counted against him, and he was not selected. Later, when his father became too old to look after him, Jack went into a mental handicap hospital, the last thing that either of his parents would have wanted. He was not happy there. The unwillingness of his parents to accept advice, to let him join a social training programme, and to persuade him to take exercise, had been a grave disadvantage to him.

Handicapped people can benefit from education and training over a very long period. For many of them, social training is as important as anything else. With help, they can develop skills that will be of great value in the house, while travelling or on holiday, and in other settings. The BBC *Let's Go* programmes give good examples of the types of social skills that can, and should, be developed. If it seems that the future of a particular handicapped person will involve his staying - at some time in the future – at a group home or a hostel, or living in a room of his own, his parents should take advice so that he can obtain the training that is appropriate. If they do not do this, then life may be much more difficult for him when the time comes that he must leave home.

It is often necessary to obtain financial advice, possibly in connection with taxation, in relation to the investment of money, or for the purpose of making a will. Accountants normally deal with tax matters, although solicitors are also competent to do this, especially in relation to capital transfer tax. Solicitors are also concerned with the making of wills and the setting-up of trusts, which are explained in Chapter 6. Whichever professional is attending to your own tax situation, it is important that he should know the special factors that apply to people who are handicapped. Mrs Renshaw went to her bank manager to discuss a short-term loan so that she could buy a car, and during the discussion with her he suggested that she should make a will and appoint the bank as her executor. He mentioned the bank's fees, but he did not tell her that they would almost certainly be a good deal more than a solicitor would charge. He also suggested that she should set up a continuing trust for the benefit of her handicapped daughter; the bank would be glad to act as trustee, he said, and its services would be available to ensure that the money was well invested. He omitted to mention, because he did not know, that the trust he had suggested would be of little use to Mrs Renshaw's daughter, as almost all the income would end in the hands of the Local Authority, the girl already having been promised a place in a nearby hostel.

The correct advice would have enabled Mrs Renshaw to compare the different costs of having a solicitor or the bank act as her executor. It would also have taken into account the fact that her daughter would at some time move into Local Authority accommodation, and a scheme on the lines mentioned in Chapter 9 should have been discussed with her. The bank manager was right to say that Mrs Renshaw's investments should be properly managed, but this could have been arranged after direct contact with a stockbroker, if she had been introduced to one. The bank would be glad to handle her tax affairs, and those of her daughter, charging a fee for doing so; but so would an accountant, and his services would be more personal to her. Banks are, of course, entirely reliable and respectable, but their officials tend to change as they are moved from place to place, following promotion. Accountants, solicitors and stockbrokers offer a more personal service, and although they can naturally retire or die, there is normally a younger member of the firm available to take their place. Nevertheless, many people in Mrs Renshaw's position do go to a bank to deal with financial matters. If, however, they are at all doubtful about any legal or tax advice they are given, they should check this with an independent professional adviser.

Assuming that you have found the right adviser, organisation, or agency, what questions should you put? Everyone knows the feeling that, after an interview, there are questions which they wish they had asked. Parents have many doubts and anxieties. It is so easy to forget the things that you want to know, and it can also happen that you misunderstand, or cannot remember, all the advice you have been given. The sensible thing to do is to write down the questions which you wish to ask. It may also help to have written a detailed account of the circumstances of your handicapped child and of his family situation. You can send this, in advance, to the person whom you will be visiting to give you advice.

To avoid forgetting what you have been told, you can ask the adviser to confirm it to you in writing. This he will certainly do if you are paying a fee for his services. If not, then take pencil and paper, make a note of what he has said, and read it back to him to make sure you have got it right. Parents who may feel foolish about doing this should remember that they are not experts, and that it is only reasonable that they should take away with them a note of what they have been told. If time is very short, then you should certainly take down a note of what has been said, even if there is no opportunity to have it fully checked.

We have seen that it is not easy to get advice, and that it may be hard to remember everything that has been said. For some people, the biggest problem is to act on the advice that they have been given. It is, after all, only advice; it is not an instruction. Some advice simply cannot be acted on, because it will cost too much money - for example, when private medical treatment is suggested. It is also quite possible that the advice may be unpalatable: Mr and Mrs Potter were not willing to accept the suggestions that had been made to them. Many parents of handicapped children have been strongly advised to allow their children to leave home, at least for short periods of time, in the knowledge that there will be some small degree of risk. Understandably, some parents are not willing to accept this advice, but they should at least consider the long-term view. If they do not act today on the advice they have been given, what will it mean, in the more distant future, for their handicapped child? We cannot blame Mr and Mrs Potter for wanting to keep Jack with them for as long as they could, but if they had been able to foresee that he would go into a mental handicap hospital, would they not have been more willing to make sure that he started to diet and to take exercise, and that he was given special training to help him live a more independent life?

It is a common experience in charitable organisations concerned with physical and mental handicaps, that many of those with whom they work have been greatly over-protected. After many years of coping with their child's every need - and having been little helped by the professions or by the statutory services - some parents cannot accept that a new approach to their child would work, or be right for him. They can imagine him suffering and protesting as he is asked to learn new skills, and they decide that it would be much better if they continued to do everything themselves. Yet they know that the day will come when they cannot go on doing this, and it is this knowledge that makes them more and more anxious as the years go by.

When Barrie Harding left school, he went to a Social Education Centre run by the Local Authority. Part of the training programme involved the staff of the Centre taking Barrie and the other trainees into a nearby market. It was not easy; Barrie and the others were mentally handicapped, and he in particular needed very close supervision. Mrs Harding learned what was happening, and decided that the risks that were being taken were too great. She told the Centre that Barrie was ill (although in fact he was as healthy as usual) and when the bus called to pick him up she did not let him go. One of the staff of the Centre visited her, in the evening, when her husband was also there. So was Barrie, watching television at the other end of the room, yet obviously aware that he was being discussed. The staff member invited Mr and Mrs Harding to visit the Centre. Mr Harding took a day off work, and they both attended on a day when Barrie was being taught the simple skill of tying his shoelaces. To their surprise, he was very successful, although this was a task which his parents had always done for him. They agreed to allow him to continue to go to the Centre, and during the following three years he was able to make a lot of progress. At the end of that time, he was transferred to a sheltered workshop, where he was trained to do a simple but useful job. In the end, the Hardings were glad that they had taken the advice they had been given, and had allowed Barrie to remain at the Education Centre.

6　Wills and Trusts

A will is not a mysterious document. It does not threaten you. It is simply a statement of what is to happen to your property when you die. There are, of course, many technical legal phrases connected with wills: the person who makes it is a 'testator' if a man, and a 'testatrix' if a woman. Those who receive the money, or other property, are the beneficiaries; the person who carries out your wishes is your executor, and if he continues to hold your property for some time, in accordance with your directions, he is known as a trustee. Legal phraseology is used in your will, because it states your wishes in a precise manner.

Precision is absolutely necessary. A man went into a stationer's shop and bought a document calling itself a 'will form'. Not wanting to pay a solicitor's charges, he decided to fill it out himself. In the space where the instructions said he should set out his wishes, he wrote the words: 'All to Mother.' He intended that his wife, whom he had always called 'Mother', should receive everything he possessed. It so happened that, when he died, his own mother was still alive. She had never liked his wife, and when she read the will she said that it was she who was entitled to the money. The widow hotly denied this claim, as her husband had told her that he had made a will leaving her everything. The result was a contested will, with large fees paid to the lawyers out of the estate, and bad feeling in the family. In the end, the judge decided in favour of the wife, but the fees of both wife and mother considerably reduced the amount of property available. The fees of the lawyers acting for the executors also had to be paid, with the result that the wife's share was greatly reduced.

Another testator, well-to-do and a successful businessman, also decided that he could do without a solicitor. He went to the local library, wrote out his own will on the basis of some forms he had found there in a book about wills, and left his large estate, worth well over £250,000, 'equally to my wife and children'. He was survived by his wife and by his three children. He had told his wife that he had left her half his property, but the executor was not sure that this was what the will said. Did it not mean, he asked, that each of the four beneficiaries should take an equal share, that is, one quarter each? There was another court application, again involving considerable expense, partly because one of the children was under eighteen years. Ultimately, the judge agreed with the executor, and each of the beneficiaries was awarded one quarter of the property. The wife only received one half of what she had expected.

Both men should have taken legal advice, and many more examples of similar cases could be given. It does not make sense to prepare your own will; you may fail to make provision for an event you cannot foresee. One of your children may die before you, leaving grandchildren who are in need; a divorce may create a situation in which it would be more sensible to create a long-term trust than to make a straight gift. Where there is a handicapped member of the family, his or her circumstances may change as time goes by, and a will should allow for this.

Wills must be in writing, or typed or printed. Most are typewritten. If possible, they should be on one sheet of paper, folded if necessary. The reason is that it would be possible to add extra sheets, after the will has been signed, if they are only pinned or stapled together. The will must be signed at the end; it will not be valid, for example, if the only signature is at the top of the first sheet, or in a margin. It is quite common for testators to sign each sheet, but there must always be a signature at the end of the will. The document should also be dated, so that there shall be no dispute if more than one will is found; a later will takes precedence over an earlier one.

The will must be witnessed. The witnesses sign their names

in the presence of the testator and of each other, and he signs in their presence. The whole process takes place while they are all in the same room together; you cannot send your will through the post and ask someone to act as a witness at a distance. Witnesses should not be people who have been given a benefit in a will, nor married to a beneficiary. The reason is that, although their signatures as witnesses are valid, they cannot receive the money or property given to them, and nor can their spouse. This rule is designed to prevent people from forging wills, or influencing a testator to give them a benefit.

It is usual to keep one's will at the solicitor's office, or at a bank. It should certainly be in a safe place, where no one can take it. People have been known to destroy wills when they realised that they would do better under an intestacy. It can be sensible to put with your will a note of all your property, but this is not legally necessary. Some people make out a list of their possessions, furniture, jewellery, books, and so on, and write against them a note of the people whom they would like to inherit them. This will only be legally valid if the will itself refers to the list and asks the executor to act on its instructions.

The first task of an executor is to see to the funeral arrangements. Having done this, he will discover any debts that are owed, and the extent of the property of the deceased person. He will know who is entitled to the property, and will tell the beneficiaries. The traditional 'reading of the will' by the family solicitor is today a very rare occasion; the beneficiaries are usually sent a copy, or receive a letter telling them what they have been given.

Before the executor is allowed access to the property left by a deceased person under a will, he must 'prove' the will to a court of law. This will not involve him in attendance in front of a judge, but he will be expected to produce the will to the High Court of Justice (Probate Division), and he will have to sign and swear a document (known as an affidavit) which says that he identifies the will and himself as the person named as executor. He 'swears' the document in front of a commissioner for oaths, and then he and the commissioner sign the will itself, usually on the first page, so as to link it with the affidavit. Court fees are paid, and after some time a probate grant is issued. This is a large official document in which is bound a copy of the will; it states that the executor is duly approved by the Court. Copies of the front page of this document, naming the executor, can be obtained from the Court, and these are shown to the bank where the deceased person kept his money, and to anyone else who may be concerned, for example the registrar of a company in which he had shares. If the deceased owned a house, then a copy of the Probate Act (i.e. the front page) will be put with the deeds. It will be needed if the house is sold. If the title to the land is 'registered' at HM Land Registry, then the executor's name will replace that of the deceased as the owner, on the official register.

Probate cannot be obtained until a payment in respect of capital transfer tax has been made. This may involve borrowing quite a large sum of money from a bank. The Government made this an essential preliminary to the grant of probate of wills, so that it could be sure of collecting its taxes. When the tax has had to be borrowed from the bank, the executor, as soon as probate has been obtained, sells enough of the assets to enable him to repay the loan. He is then in a position to turn some or all of the rest of the deceased's property, for example money deposited with a building society, into cash, and this he puts in his executor's account at the bank. He then pays any other debts, and the funeral expenses, settles the cost of administering the estate, and transfers the remaining assets to the people entitled under the will. If the will contains a 'charging clause', then the executor will be able to charge a fee for his work. This normally happens if he, as a solicitor, has been appointed as sole executor, or as joint executor with another member of the family. If there is no 'charging clause', then the executor is not entitled to a fee for himself, although he is of course allowed to place the administration of the estate in the hands of a solicitor, whose fee is a proper deduction from the value of the estate.

The testator may have given some cash legacies, e.g. gifts of jewellery. He may then have 'bequeathed', or given, the rest of his estate, known as the 'residue', to one person, or have divided it among several. The executor draws up a detailed account, pays out or transfers the assets and obtains receipts, and that is an end of the matter, unless there are continuing trusts to be administered.

It is of course when we come to trusts that handicapped children are likely to be considered. Most people, when making their wills, give their property outright to their wife or husband, or to their grown-up children. It may be different when the child is handicapped, especially if he is mentally handicapped; to give him property in his own name may not make sense, if he cannot understand it. In the first place, people may try to take advantage of his ignorance, and deprive him of his property. Secondly, if the Court of Protection is brought in to guard the property, there may be unnecessary expense and delay.

The alternative is to create a trust. The property, whether money, furniture or a house, is put into the name of a trustee (probably the same person who has been appointed as executor of the will). The trustee is its legal owner, but he cannot use it for his own benefit; he must deal with it as instructed in the will. Typically, the will says that the income on the property is to be used to benefit the handicapped person; it also provides that the property itself (known as the 'capital' of the trust) may also be spent for the beneficiary, in the discretion of the trustee. The intention is that the handicapped beneficiary will have extra comforts, and if a holiday, or some piece of equipment, such as a video-recorder or a wheelchair, is needed, it can be paid for.

Some trusts give the trustee no discretion to use capital for the beneficiary, in which case it will eventually pass on to someone else, on the death of the beneficiary. The people to whom the capital is eventually given are known as the 'residuary beneficiaries'. They may be the brothers and sisters of the handicapped person, or their surviving children. Trusts may be drawn up in a very wide variety of ways, according to the wishes of the testator. They can be made to last for eighty years or so, but most are designed to come to an end earlier than that. Many trusts exist under which the trustees have a wide discretion to give income and capital, or both, to one or more of a large number of beneficiaries. These are known as 'discretionary trusts'. A man of property can give his estate to his trustees (there will probably be two or three of them) upon trust to pay the income to his wife while she is alive, and then keep it to benefit his children and grandchildren, as seems best. He is giving the trustees the right to make decisions that he would have made, had he been alive.

One can see that the choice of trustees is vital. They are not only trusted to preserve the property and see that it is well invested. They may also find themselves having to make complex decisions on the competing claims of a large number of people. The testator must therefore choose the trustees very carefully. In the first place, he will naturally select people who are younger than himself, for he wants them to live long enough to carry out the trusts for the benefit of his family. Secondly, he will want to be sure that they are entirely trustworthy in the personal sense, and that they know his family; he may very well tell them of his intentions, and explain his hopes for the future, knowing that they will carry out his wishes.

When discretionary trusts are to be set up, the most sensible appointment as trustee is probably a near relation, one who does not receive a benefit under the will but who knows the family well. He or she should be appointed jointly with a professional person, such as the family solicitor. Difficulties may arise if one of the trustees can receive a benefit under the will, so it is usually best to avoid this. Banks advertise their services as trustees, but they do not say that their charges tend to be much higher than those of professional people, nor that the charges they make are usually based on the value of the trust assets, irrespective of the amount of work they do. They may make an annual charge calculated by reference to the value of a house in which a widow is living, which a professional trustee does not normally do. His charge is based on the amount of work actually done. Banks rightly claim that they cannot die, but they do not stress the fact that the officials in a bank's trustee department quite often change their jobs and move, with the result that the family may have to get to know a new official whom they have never met and who knows little of their history, their personalities or their needs. The best trustees are friends and advisers, who will themselves appoint new trustees, if and when the time comes for them to retire.

Of course, if a simple trust is being set up, which provides for income to be paid to a handicapped person, then there is no need to appoint several independent trustees. When there is no wide class of beneficiaries, but only one, then there is nothing to prevent the testator from appointing two of his non-handicapped children as trustees of the property. It is usually best to have two trustees, rather than one. Trusts do not have to be set up by will. There is nothing to prevent a parent, or some other relative, from creating a trust during his lifetime, provided he can afford to do without the money that he is 'settling' in the trust. He can later add more property to the trust during his life, or by his will, and so can other members of the family.

A valuable tax concession was given in the Finance Act 1975 (Paragraph 19 of Schedule 5). Under it, no capital transfer tax is payable in respect of discretionary trusts set up only or mainly for the benefit of mentally disabled persons. Under the Finance Act 1977, this concession was extended (by Section 51 of the Act) to all beneficiaries receiving the Attendance Allowance. Unfortunately, regulations that concern Supplementary Benefits and Local Authority accommodation, have largely nullified these valuable concessions.

A word about investment: it is not normally sensible for trustees to keep property in exactly the same form in which they receive it. The will usually gives them wide powers to vary the form of investment. They may decide, for example, to sell a house or some other property, add to it the cash that is available after paying debts and funeral expenses, and obtain the advice of a stockbroker on the best way to invest the money so as to protect the capital, yet at the same time provide a reasonably high income. The trustees' duty is to review the investment of the trust funds regularly, and to consider what is right, taking into account the interests of all the beneficiaries. For example, while a widow is alive, they may very well see to it that the income on the funds is fairly high, to ensure that her needs are met. After she dies, though, it may be sensible to reduce the income by reinvesting the capital in such a way that it will grow steadily over the years, rather than remaining static. In making these difficult decisions, the trustees may want to talk with the beneficiaries and with those who are caring for them, if they are handicapped. Then they will take professional advice on what it is best to do, bearing in mind the needs of all those involved. It can be seen that the task of a trustee is onerous, and one should select one's trustee carefully, for he has an important and difficult job to do. In one's will, it is possible to provide that a trustee is paid a fee for the responsibility he is taking on.

Parents of a handicapped child have a special problem when making their wills. Mr and Mrs Hamilton have three children: John is 28, married, and with two children of his own; he lives over 100 miles from his parents and has a reasonably good job, with prospects of promotion. Sarah, their daughter, is 26 and has one child; unfortunately, her marriage broke up and she is living with her parents, as is her young son. The third child of Mr and Mrs Hamilton is Bruce who is mentally handicapped; he can manage to dress himself, go to the toilet and eat meals without help, and at 20 years, is bigger than both his mother and his father. Each day he is taken to a nearby Adult Training Centre, and returns about 5.00 pm. Over the years he has never been expected to do much around the house, because he tends to break things. He has become used to having more or less everything done for him. He likes Sarah's little boy and plays happily with him.

Mr and Mrs Hamilton have been talking about their wills. They have just finished paying off the mortgage on the house and it is worth quite a lot of money. They also have some life insurance, and Mrs Hamilton's mother has just died, leaving her a cottage near Bournemouth. Although they are certainly not rich, the property they own is valuable; it is not available in cash, but they have worked out that if they died, a large amount of capital transfer tax would have to be paid. When they saw their solicitor, they came away without deciding what they wanted to put in their wills; it was all far more complicated than they thought. Mrs Hamilton certainly wanted Bruce to be cared for, but she also thought that John and Sarah should receive their fair share of the family property; having a handicapped brother had meant that life had not been very easy for them and Mrs Hamilton did not want them to be deprived of property; she therefore does not want to give everything to Bruce, or to put it all in trust for him. At the same time, she realises that, if anything happened to her, Sarah's needs would be great; she does not receive much maintenance from her former husband and depends very much on her mother and father. She would like to re-marry and, as she is an attractive girl, the chances are that this will happen. At present, though, much of her time is taken up with her little boy.

The family solicitor had some shocks for Mr and Mrs Hamilton when they went to see him. He told them about the effects of the rules relating to Supplementary Benefits and Local Authority homes, which will be described below. Mr and Mrs Hamilton are not at all certain what to do. One third of their property, they think, should go direct to John. They are not so sure about Sarah; she has never been able to manage money, and they are certain that if property came into her hands, she would spend it unwisely. When their solicitor explained that Sarah's share could be put in trust for her and the income paid to her, with the trustees having power to give her some capital as well (in their discretion), this seemed very sensible. They naturally thought that the same arrangement could be made for Bruce and were worried when the solicitor explained how difficult it would be to achieve this. At present, they have only reached the point of deciding that it would probably be best to make John and their solicitor the executors and trustees of their wills. Fortunately, John and Sarah get on well together and she has often looked to him to advise her; they are not at all likely to fall out because he will have control of her share, as a trustee. On the contrary, she is likely to trust his advice, and his judgment.

The difficulties that Mr and Mrs Hamilton face, in making provision for Bruce, stem from regulations laid down by Parliament, affecting people who receive benefits from the State, or from Local Government. As a result of the regulations, no Supplementary Benefit can be paid to people who own a minimum amount of money or property (at present £3,000). Other regulations enable a Local Authority to make a substantial charge for providing residential accommodation for someone who needs it.

People who are helped by the State, or by Local Government, are receiving money from the ratepayer, or the taxpayer, or both. The idea of the regulations is that those who can afford to pay their own living expenses should not expect the rest of us to put our hands in our pockets on their behalf. This is of course a political issue: some people say that any person who is handicapped should be cared for by the rest of the community; others claim that everyone, handicapped or not, should use up their own resources before the taxpayers and the ratepayers have to support them. The issue is clear-cut when one is considering someone who is not handicapped and who has plenty of his own resources; why should the rest of us support him? The argument is not so clear when we consider a handicapped person who is unable to look after himself, and who needs extra comforts beyond those which are provided by the State.

Aside from politics, which must be left to special pressure groups and organisations which campaign on behalf of handicapped people, we can only deal with the law as it is, not as we would wish it to be. The detailed Regulations are set out in Appendix I, which contains an extract from Statutory Instrument No. 1527 of 1981. Here, we are concerned with their effect. In previous years, much discretion was left with the officials of the Department of Health and Social Security, who were allowed to decide if benefits ought to be reduced when the person receiving them had money of his own, or was a beneficiary under a trust. New and more restrictive regulations were introduced by the Government in 1980. The element of discretion left to the officials of the DHSS has been eliminated, with the result that any person with capital resources of more than £3,000, or receiving income from a trust which is worth more than that amount, immediately ceases to be entitled to any Supplementary Benefit at all.

The 'capital resources' that may, if they add up to more than £3,000 in value, bring an end to Supplementary Benefits, include:

- Money, in cash or deposited with a bank or a building society, or in a Post Office Savings Bank.
- National Savings Certificates and Premium Bonds.
- Stocks and shares, and other investments.
- The surrender value of life assurance policies.
- The value of house property and land, less deductions for a mortgage and for the cost of a sale, *unless* the person claiming the benefit is normally living in the house.
- Interest which has been saved for a longer period of time than it took to earn; for example, if interest is added to a savings account for a six months period, it is counted as capital if it is not spent within the next six months.
- Valuable possessions, such as an oil painting.
- Anything bought with the deliberate intention of reducing the amount of capital so as to qualify for the benefit.

If the home in which the person receiving benefit lives is up for sale, or if the money from its sale is held to buy another home for him, then this is not counted as a capital resource. If the person goes into Local Authority accommodation for a short period, then there is no pressure on him to sell his home, but after he has been away for a substantial period and it appears that he is not likely to return, then the Authorities will often bring pressure to bear to sell the house. They have no legal power to force a sale, but they can build up a large debt – by way of their charge for residential accommodation – and can enforce this when the house is eventually sold. In many cases, this power effectively forces a sale, because of the growing amount of the debt.

The figure of £3,000 as a 'cut-off' limit for benefits was set in 1983, and it is likely that it will be adjusted from time to time, to keep pace with inflation. Further adjustments may also be made, in response to political pressure. At the time of writing, however, the effect of the regulations is to bring to an end all entitlement to Supplementary Benefit, until the money has been spent so as to bring its total down below £3,000. Many trusts have been reduced in this way, over a period of years, from as much as £10,000 to the 'cut-off' figure of £3,000.

This does not mean that all State Benefits are withdrawn. A handicapped person may be entitled to Attendance Allowance and Mobility Allowance, and other benefits (See Chapter 3). He will certainly continue to receive the Non-Contributory Invalidity Pension, if he can produce medical evidence that he is unable to work. At present, the level of Supplementary Benefit is £27.25 a week, and there is an addition for people who are living at home but are not householders, of £3.10 a week, plus a Heating Allowance of £5.05 a week (if receiving Mobility Allowance and/or Attendance Allowance). So the Supplementary Benefit, the Rent Addition and the Heating Allowance can come to £35.40 a week. The Non-Contributory Invalidity Pension is £20.45 per week, leaving a potential difference of

£14.95 a week. All these figures are of course subject to variation from time to time.

Parents who are sure that their child will continue to live in a house he owns, or in a house bought with the funds of a trust of which he is a beneficiary, can go ahead and create such a trust. There is of course a risk: if the handicapped person has to leave the house - for example, because his condition has deteriorated - then it becomes a 'capital resource' the value of which must enter into the calculation of his means; he may then lose the Supplementary Benefit, as explained above.

Mr and Mrs Hamilton certainly cannot be sure that Bruce will live in their present home, or in a home bought with money they could leave him. They therefore face a considerable dilemma. If they put more than £3,000 in trust for Bruce, is it going to bring any real benefit to him? There must come a point at which a very large sum of money, put into trust, would provide Bruce with extra benefits, but how can they calculate that sum today? There is no simple answer that will apply to every family with a handicapped child. The circumstances of each handicapped person must be considered separately. These are some of the more important elements to be considered in reaching a decision:

- The degree of his handicap.
- The State Benefits to which he is now entitled.
- The accommodation that is likely to be provided for him when the time comes.
- The amount of money available to put into the trust, the income this will produce, and the tax that will have to be paid on this income.
- The needs of other members of the family, for example, his brothers and sisters.

At present, any sum less than £12,500 may not result in much additional benefit to the handicapped person. This figure is based on the following assumptions:

Assumed income on £12,500,
   put in trust, at 9% per
   annum (this rate would of
   course alter if interest rates
   generally are changed)

                         £1,125 per annum

Less Tax at 30% (subject
   to any Personal Allowances
   he may be able to claim)   __338__
                          £787 per annum

The weekly equivalent of this sum of £787 is £15.13, which is much the same as the difference between the Supplementary Benefit and other Benefits, and the Non-Contributory Invalidity Pension.

We have already seen, in Chapter 3, that it can make very good sense for a person to transfer to the Non-Contributory Invalidity Pension. If Bruce did this at present, he would be paid £20.45 per week by way of pension, and another £6.80 a week by way of Supplementary Benefit, bringing him up to £27.25 a week. As it happens, he does not receive either the Attendance Allowance or the Mobility Allowance, because his handicap is not serious enough to justify the payment of either. If a trust came into existence with a value of more than £3,000, Bruce being a beneficiary, his entitlement to the £20.45 would continue without any interruption, but he would lose the extra £6.80 per week.

Like any other parents in this situation, Mr and Mrs Hamilton get out their pocket calculator. If they put £6,000 in trust for Bruce, they calculate, and if this gives a return of 9%, then his income will be £540 a year. If Income Tax at 30% has to be deducted, this will be reduced to £378 a year, which is a little better than the difference between Supplementary Benefit and Non-Contributory Invalidity Pension, i.e. £353.60 (£6.80 × 52). If Bruce would not have to pay any tax, then there would be a greater benefit to him.

They find this reasonably satisfactory, but then they realise that if they put a sum of £6,000 in Government Stocks, so as to bring in the income of £540 a year, there is no protection against inflation; the real value of the income may drop as the years go by, leaving less and less money available for Bruce's benefit. This is a problem that has been suffered by anyone who has had to live on a fixed income. They therefore decide that it might be more sensible to aim for an income of 6%, and that the money in the trust should be invested in the shares of public companies, perhaps through Unit Trusts. At this rate of interest, £9,000 will be needed to produce £540 a year.

Is it all really worth while at this level, they wonder? After all, the real benefit they will be giving Bruce is only the difference between the income on the trust, and the loss of Supplementary Benefit he will suffer. Does it really make sense for them to put £9,000 aside, when the actual benefit to him may be as little as £1 a week? They look again at their own assets, including their house, their life insurance policies, car, jewellery, furniture and other belongings, and come to the conclusion that they are worth about £48,000. If one third of this was put in trust for Bruce, this would amount to £16,000. This could be invested to bring in about £20 a week, subject to income tax. At this stage, and bearing in mind the needs of their other children, John and Sarah, they decide that it would be worth while to create a trust in favour of Bruce.

There will be many parents, reading these words and calculations, who will be put off. Some may be so discouraged that they will be tempted to give up the attempt. The truth is that, because the regulations on Supplementary Benefit exist, there is no way of avoiding the mathematics, if some kind of benefit is to be secured for a handicapped child who survives his parents. Fortunately, professional help is available. Mr and Mrs Hamilton's solicitor will be able to check their calculations and, taking into account the important elements mentioned above, will advise them.

Unfortunately, we have by no means come to the end of the

difficulties facing Mr and Mrs Hamilton, because they are not at all certain what is going to happen to Bruce when they die. It would not be possible for their son John to take Bruce into his own home, and it is very doubtful whether Sarah could, or would want to, look after him. Inevitably, it seems that he will have to go into some kind of Local Authority accommodation. There is a large hostel in the town where he lives, and it is the only one available in the neighbourhood. Mr and Mrs Hamilton are not at all happy about this idea: the hostel has not got a particularly good reputation, but they see no alternative to it.

This has a crucial effect on the plans they are making for their wills, because there are regulations in force which enable a Local Authority to levy a charge on residents who are living in their residential accommodation. Just as the State expects people to look after themselves by using their own resources, so do the Local Authorities. Under the terms of Part III of the National Assistance Act 1948, and the Homeless Persons Act 1977, extracts from which are set out in Appendix II, Local Authorities are legally obliged to provide some residential accommodation for those who are handicapped. The Authorities normally carry out this obligation by setting up hostels or group homes, as we have seen in Chapter 4. If a handicapped person is living in such accommodation and has capital resources of his own, or is the beneficiary of a trust under which both income and capital can be used for his benefit, then the Local Authority can call for a contribution towards the cost of providing him with a home. If it is only the income from a trust to which he is entitled, then the contribution can come only from that income, and not from the capital of the trust. The result may well be that, in Bruce's case, all the income from the trust which his parents are thinking of creating will have to be paid to the Local Authority.

At present, the 'cut-off' limit for contributions to Local Authorities is fixed at only £1,200 capital, a lower limit than applies to Supplementary Benefits. For every £100 of capital in excess of £1,200, the annual amount payable to the Local

Authority is £26. (See Schedule I of the Supplementary Benefits Act 1976.) So, if Mr and Mrs Hamilton do in fact create a trust for Bruce with a value of £16,000, the payment to the Local Authority would be £3,848 a year, or £74 a week.

In fact, the powers of Local Authorities are very wide in fixing the charges they are allowed to make. These powers are set out in Paragraph 2 (5) of Schedule 8 to the National Health Service Act 1977, which empowers them to make 'such charges (if any) as the Authority consider reasonable, having regard to the means of those persons.' There is therefore no restriction on what the Authorities may claim, but a great many of them base their charge on the formula mentioned above.

In one London Borough, a widow left all the money she had to a friend, whom she appointed executor and trustee of her will. She directed that it should be used for the benefit of her handicapped daughter. When she died, the girl went to a home run by the Borough, which learned of the provisions in the will. The Borough's officials persuaded the executor to invest all the money left by the widow, which was a little over £8,000, in a loan to the Borough itself. The Borough then paid itself the interest, and kept the girl in one of its group homes. It also made a charge on the capital of £8,000, which before long was reduced to only £1,200. A local social worker, whom the widow had told of the gift which she hoped would help her daughter, protested that the girl was receiving no extra benefit whatever, in spite of her mother's will. However, because the social worker was employed by the Borough's Social Services Department (which levied the charge on the money), she was frightened to publicise the case.

Mr and Mrs Hamilton have gone back to their pocket calculator. They discover that the present fees charged by the Local Authority for the hostel are £130 a week, or over £6,760 a year. Even if the share they leave Bruce is as high as £25,000, this will still not be enough to pay the Local Authority's fees, and there will certainly be no money left over for extra benefits for Bruce. Admittedly, the Non-Contributory Invalidity Pension will be available to reduce the cost, but they find themselves thinking that it is really not worth while putting so large a sum aside for Bruce when it seems that he will receive almost no benefit from it. They talk about the possibility of giving the trustees of their wills a power to spend capital for Bruce's benefit, but they discard this idea, as it will only increase the money available to meet the Local Authority charge.

After a great deal of thought, Mr and Mrs Hamilton go back to see their solicitor. He checks all their calculations and considers the tax situation in detail. He agrees with them that, as Bruce is almost certain to have to go into a Local Authority hostel, there seems to be no way of creating a trust which would be of any benefit to him. They decide to set up a small trust for him in their wills, but they limit this to £3,000. They tell their solicitor that they wish to divide the rest of their money between John and Sarah; John is to have his half absolutely, but Sarah's is to be held in trust for her, and will ultimately go to her children. This is one solution, but they do have other options, which are explained in Chapter 9.

Many parents face exactly the dilemma that Mr and Mrs Hamilton have had to consider. If they have other children who are not handicapped, they often decide to give everything to them, in the hope that they will help their handicapped brother or sister as and when necessary. There is a major problem here, however: if the property is given to the other children, or indeed to any other relative or friend, on the understanding that it will be used for the benefit of the handicapped child, then this understanding actually creates a legally binding trust. The result can be the total loss of Supplementary Benefit, and a charge for Local Authority Accommodation.

It is sometimes said, when trustees have a complete discretion to give income or capital to several beneficiaries, including a handicapped beneficiary, that they can simply refuse to help him, whatever the effect of the trust's existence may have on his Supplementary Benefits or on fees charged for

Local Authority accommodation. This is true. The regulations do not contain any power to force trustees to make payments to one of a number of beneficiaries. The difficulty is that many families and trustees fear that, if they decline to make payments on behalf of a handicapped person, he may suffer a considerable disadvantage, either by being discharged from the home where he is living, or transferred to some other, and far less suitable, place. For this reason, they may be inclined to make the payments to the Local Authority, on behalf of the handicapped beneficiary, to save him from suffering and to ensure he stays in a place where he is reasonably happy.

Another concern of parents is that, if they make no provision for the benefit of their handicapped child, an attempt will be made to 'upset' their will. If such a claim were made, it would have to be through the Court of Protection, on behalf of the handicapped person. It is unlikely that a relative would call upon the Court of Protection to act in this way, but it is possible that a Local Authority might do so. The aim of the Authority, of course, would be to achieve an alteration of the will so that the handicapped person would receive money, and would in turn be legally obliged to pay this money over to the Authority.

The intention of the legislation, the Inheritance (Provision for Family and Dependants) Act 1975, is to benefit individuals who are dependent on a relative who fails to provide for them. For example, if a wife is left nothing by her husband, she will have a claim under the Act, and can 'upset' the will. The Act, however, was certainly not passed for the benefit of Local Authorities. If the result of changing a will, therefore, will merely be to benefit an Authority, it is unlikely in the extreme that a judge will alter its provisions. In one instance, the father of a mentally handicapped girl gave all his property to the local Mencap Society, but nothing to his handicapped daughter. The Local Authority sought to upset the will, hoping to obtain money towards the fees it wished to charge for looking after the girl. The local Mencap Society disputed the claim, saying that the father had clearly intended to give it the money, knowing full well that if he gave it to his daughter it would not bring her a substantial benefit. The Court of Protection was brought into the case, but in fact it never came to court because it was settled between the people concerned, with the help of the Court of Protection. A sum of £3,000 was set aside in trust for the daughter, this being the amount that would not prevent her from obtaining Supplementary Benefit. The rest of the money went to the local Mencap Society.

This compromise seems to be reasonably fair. It is at least probable that a judge would decide that enough provision should be made for a handicapped dependent relative to ensure that he does in fact receive some benefit from the parents' property. It therefore makes sense for parents to create a £3,000 trust under their wills in favour of their handicapped child. A trust is better than an outright gift, for it leaves the trustees with the power to give benefits to the handicapped child, and will not involve an application to the Court of Protection. There are some notes in Appendix II on the case of *Re E (deceased), E v E*, which was decided in 1966.

Clearly there will be some parents who will seek to impose a moral, though not a legal, obligation on their family to provide for the handicapped child. We can imagine them saying something like this to their other children:

'We are going to give you the whole of our property between you, and are leaving your handicapped brother only a relatively small amount. We are not imposing any legally binding trust or obligation on you at all, but we naturally hope that you will always be concerned for his welfare and happiness.'

It may be, of course, that the brothers and sisters will in fact give practical and financial help to their brother when the time comes, and they may use the money they have inherited from their parents to do this. If they make fixed and regular payments, then it is at least possible that the Department of Health and Social Security, or the Local Authority, may claim that there is in fact a secret trust in operation, one that has not been written down, but merely communicated by word of mouth. A secret trust of this kind is nonetheless a trust, and will be caught by the regulations concerning Supplementary Benefit and Local Authority accommodation.

Many parents are of course content to rely on their other children to act in a responsible way, even though there is no question of a trust being imposed, secret or otherwise. Even then, though, there are problems: money given to another child belongs to him or her absolutely. It will suffer capital gains tax and capital transfer tax in his hands; income from the money will have to bear income tax at whatever rate he must pay. If a non-handicapped child dies before his handicapped brother or sister, then his money goes to the people entitled under his will, and these may not include the handicapped person. In addition, if the non-handicapped brother or sister gets into financial difficulties, or is involved in a divorce action, then all his or her money is available for division to his creditors, or as part of the divorce settlement. In an age when one marriage in three or four is breaking up, this risk is very real.

There is of course one category of handicapped people who are unaffected by the regulations described above: those who are living in hospital. They do not receive Supplementary Benefit as such, although they are given a small amount of pocket money. They are not living in Local Authority accommodation, because of course the hospitals are part of the National Health Service, so the rules for residential charges do not affect them. For them, even a very large trust would not result in payment of money to the State or to the Local Council; yet it often happens that there is little that money can buy for them. On the other hand, if a trust is created to give additional benefits to a handicapped person in hospital, it should be realised that there is still the possibility that, if he were to leave hospital and go to live in a group home or a hostel run by a Local Authority, a charge would then have to be paid. Since the publication of the document entitled *Care in the Community* by the Department of Health & Social Security, it is now public policy to transfer handicapped people from hospitals to community homes. The pace of this transfer is accelerating, thus bringing an increasing number of people within the scope of the regulations.

A very small minority of people may be able to afford to place in a trust a sum of money which is so large that it will provide enough income each year to keep a handicapped person in a private home. Such a trust would be framed so that it avoided the payment of any capital transfer tax, a considerable advantage in the case of rich families. It seems, however, that the amount of money involved, taking into account the high rates of income tax that would have to be paid, would exceed £100,000, and there are very few people indeed who can contemplate the creation of so large a trust.

Faced with so many frustrating and alarming obstacles, the parents of handicapped children may well feel that the regulations approved by Parliament have been designed to make life even harder for them and their handicapped child than it already is. All is not necessarily lost, however, and in the remaining chapters of this book we shall consider alternatives, such as the Mencap Homes Foundation, the Mencap City Foundation, the Mencap Trustee Visitors Service, and the provision made by other national and local charities.

7 Property

Handicapped people can own property, just like anyone else. Those who are not mentally handicapped can, and do, manage their property, their home, and everything else that belongs to them. The laws of property apply to them, and the fact of their handicap is irrelevant. Of course, the fact that they are handicapped may expose them to some special risks - it is relatively easy to steal something from a blind person - but they have the same rights and responsibilities as other people. It is a source of great irritation to handicapped people that they are sometimes treated as if they are socially incompetent and lack understanding of what is going on around them.

The situation is often different in the case of mentally handicapped people. Some are able to manage money and can understand what it means to own a house, a car, or a piece of furniture. Mental handicap is a matter of degree, and it has been discovered in recent years that many mentally handicapped people can manage things better than their families believe is possible; the experience of independent living has given them the chance to develop their understanding. It is vitally important for the parents of mentally handicapped children to create every possible opportunity for them to learn about the way the world works, and to understand money and possessions. If they do not do this, the time may come when their child is denied the chance of a more independent life.

William Green, a boy with Down's Syndrome, was never given the chance to handle money, except a few coins which he took to a Gateway Club he visited in the evenings, to pay for tea and biscuits. His parents always made sure he had exactly the right amount of cash, and put it in an envelope which he took with him on the bus. Although he could sign his name and manage himself very well, William always had everything done for him. As his parents grew old, they felt it would be best for him to move into a new hostel that the Local Council had built, quite near their home. Sadly, when William was assessed, it turned out that he could not really cope with a room of his own, nor with the simple problems of paying rent and doing his share of the housework at the hostel. As a result, another young man was preferred to him as a resident, and William stayed on at home. In fact, he could quite well have been trained to do these things, given time and encouragement, and would have been happy at the hostel, because two of his friends had moved there. His future is now bleak, as there are no plans for other homes or hostels in the area.

People like William should be allowed to handle money, provided they can understand what it means and can be trained to control it sensibly. They should not, of course, be given control over large sums, as there is always the danger that unscrupulous people may try to take it from them. Much depends on the degree of handicap, but we should start with the assumption that a handicapped person can be trained to accept some responsibility for managing what is his.

It is all a matter of degree. William could have been taught to manage small sums of money and to handle a Post Office Savings Account; he could not have operated a bank account, signed cheques or kept a note of the balance of money in the bank. It is obvious, however, that there are some people whose handicap is so severe that they cannot understand, let alone manage, property or money, in which case it is best that they should not become owners at all. If ownership cannot be avoided, for example when a handicapped person receives a benefit under the will of a distant relative, then it will be necessary to seek the help of the Court of Protection.

THE COURT OF PROTECTION

The Court of Protection exists to manage the property of people who are unable to do so themselves. So when a man or woman owns money, a house, stocks and shares, or other possessions, the only way to deal with them may be to apply to the Court. Although it has all the powers of any other court, it operates quite informally: there is no judge in a wig, no benches, no reporters, no witness box and no dock. If it were not for the legal forms to be filled in, headed 'COURT OF PROTECTION . . . In The Matter Of . . .', one might think, when going to the Court, that one is visiting an ordinary office.

The great majority of cases that come to the Court involve the property of people who have become senile through old age, but the Court also handles cases involving handicapped people. There are, of course, many forms of handicap which do not prevent a person from dealing with his own money and other property, but when a man or woman has sustained brain-damage, or is in some other way mentally handicapped, the Court has an essential role. If it did not exist, there would be no way of handling the property of people who cannot manage it for themselves.

Whenever possible, matters should be arranged so that mentally handicapped people do not come into the ownership of property, unless of course they have enough understanding to appreciate the meaning of ownership. Unfortunately, however, mentally handicapped people do sometimes inherit property under the will of a grandparent or other relative, or as the result of an intestacy. If the surviving parent of a mentally handicapped person dies without making a will, then his child will inherit a share of his property, and the Court of Protection will inevitably have to be brought in. It has been said that, if there are Ten Commandments for most people, there are eleven for the parents of a mentally handicapped child, the eleventh being: 'Thou Shalt Not Die Intestate.' Not only will an intestacy force the family to apply to the Court of Protection, but the handicapped person may very well lose his Supplementary Benefits, and may have to pay large sums of his money to a Local Authority for residential accommodation, as explained in Chapter 6.

Another reason why the Court of Protection is a very necessary institution is that there are always people around who are glad of the opportunity to obtain control of the money of someone who cannot manage it for himself. The Court prevents this from happening, but it is much more sensible to arrange matters so that the handicapped person never comes into the ownership of property at all, in which case there is no need to go to the Court.

The way the Court of Protection usually works is to appoint a 'Receiver' of the handicapped person's property, that is, someone who manages it on his behalf, but under the supervision of the Court. Usually, the Receiver is a near relative, a parent, or a brother or sister, who has applied to the Court for its help. A relative can make a personal application by writing to the Court, which replies through the post, sending a series of forms. One of these is an affidavit, that is, a document which has to be 'sworn' before a commissioner for oaths. Another document is a medical certificate, which has to be signed by a doctor; the Court will never make an order dealing with property unless it is absolutely satisfied that the owner is incapable of dealing with it himself. Medical evidence is always required. The Court also often requires a security bond from the Receiver, but it will give clear instructions as to how to get one.

While it is perfectly possible to make one's own application to become a Receiver for a handicapped relative, including a son or daughter, most people ask a solicitor to make the application for them. His fee is of course payable from the property of the handicapped person. The solicitor can also give legal advice, which the relative may find very helpful; he can obtain the order from the Court, and then 'register' it with a bank, a building society, the Post Office, or anyone else who needs to see it, as authority for the Receiver to manage the handicapped person's property.

The Receiver can, when authorised by the Court, do a wide range of things: he can, and indeed must, maintain any property belonging to the handicapped person, and also insure it; he will operate bank accounts, review investments, handle income tax, and of course arrange for holidays, extra comforts, clothes and so on. One administrative burden he must usually shoulder is the submission of an annual account to the Court, giving details of all financial transactions, although in some cases the Court will be satisfied with an annual enquiry, rather than a set of accounts. The accounts must be accompanied by vouchers, receipts, dividend counterfoils, and so on. It is the same sort of document as a yearly tax return. A good deal of time and trouble may be involved each year, and one can well understand why people try to avoid having to apply to the Court unless it is absolutely unavoidable. Unfortunately, Legal Aid is not available for applications to the Court, presumably because the handicapped person's property is available to pay legal fees.

It has often been said that the procedures of the Court are very slow, and take too much time. Recent steps have been taken to ensure a reasonably quick response to an application, and it is now normal for an appointment to be fixed by the Court within four weeks of receiving the formal request for its help. Even so, the process does take time, especially if there are any complications. A short procedure is available if the value of the property involved is not more than £5,000. Contrary to popular belief, there is no lower limit of value; the Court can act on applications to deal with quite small sums of money. Moreover, it does have the power to act very quickly, within days or even hours, if a case is urgent. It powers are very wide indeed, and it can make a will for a mentally handicapped person.

Fees have to be paid for all applications to the Court of Protection, and they are levied every year, not just on the occasion of the first application to the Court. They are based on the 'clear annual income' of the handicapped person, that is, what is available for him to spend after tax and other deductions. The fees are calculated as follows:

Clear Annual Income		Fee
Exceeding	*Not Exceeding*	
Nil	£ 1,000	None
£ 1,000	£ 2,000	£ 75
£ 2,000	£ 3,000	£150
£ 3,000	£ 5,000	£225
£ 5,000	£ 7,000	£375
£ 7,000	£10,000	£600
£10,000	£20,000	£850

If the clear annual income is over £20,000, the fee is £850 plus 5 per cent of the amount by which the income exceeds £20,000.

Roger White was injured in a motor-cycle accident when he was eighteen. His head was badly damaged and he was no longer able to work, even after he had left hospital. Sadly, he was quite unable to understand ordinary business or money matters, although at the time of his accident he had passed his 'A' levels with good grades, and had been offered a place at a university. It took a long time to obtain an award of damages for him, because it was not easy to prove that the accident had been the fault of the other driver. It was three years before an award was finally made, amounting to £35,000. Roger was unable to sign cheques or make decisions, so the family solicitors, who had been handling the case for damages, applied to the Court of Protection for a decision on what was to be done with the £35,000.

Roger was living at home with his parents after the accident. For much of the time he was in a wheelchair, although able to walk short distances, and he could manage a few things for himself. There was some discussion about who should be appointed as the Receiver. Until 1983, it was possible to appoint the Official Solicitor, a Court officer, but this no longer applies. Instead, the Court of Protection has the power to appoint one of its own officers, who is known as the 'Principal of the Management Division of the Court of

Protection'. He charges a 'Commencement Fee' of £200. For this and other reasons, Roger's father decided to apply himself to be appointed as Receiver, and the Court agreed to this. The Court, by which is meant the 'Master' who was considering the case, approved the suggestion by Mr White that several thousands of pounds should be spent on special equipment for his home, which would help his parents move Roger up and down stairs, and bath and feed him. Other sums were spent on clothes and holidays, and on the fees of a private physiotherapist who helped Roger to move his limbs more effectively. All this expenditure had first to be authorised by the Court, after it had considered the wisdom of the proposals.

After the money had been spent on equipment and other items, Roger was still left with over £27,000. He ceased to be entitled to Supplementary Benefit (see Chapter 6), but he was able to claim the Non-Contributory Invalidity Pension, and also the Attendance Allowance. The Court authorised his father to obtain advice from a stockbroker, and as a result Roger's money was invested in good stocks and shares, bringing in an income, before tax, of about £2,000 a year. This was used for his benefit, as were the Invalidity Pension and the Attendance Allowance.

When Roger's parents die, or become too old to look after him, all this income will continue to be available for his benefit and his £27,000 capital will be preserved. However, if he goes into a Local Authority home, the £27,000 will be steadily reduced by the fees payable to the Local Authority. It may even sink as low as £1,200, for the reasons given in Chapter 6. The Court of Protection will probably appoint Roger's brother to be Receiver, in place of his father, when the time comes.

Roger never made a will, but this is something the Court may do for him. As he has only the one brother, and no other close relatives except his parents, the Court is likely to approve a will which gives Roger's money to his parents, or, if he outlives them, to his brother Brian. Let us suppose that, in time, this does happen; Roger may very well survive his parents, but his expectation of life is less than normal because of the accident. This has led Brian to consider whether he would then take him into his own home, or perhaps move into their parents' home, where all the equipment exists to help Roger. Thinking it over, Brian realises that if Roger does go into a Local Authority home, his money will eventually disappear, because of the payment of residential fees, at £130 a week or maybe more. The result could be that, even if Brian inherits everything under Roger's will, there may not be much left when he dies.

On the death of the parents, Brian and his wife will have a difficult decision to make. If they take Roger into their own home, or if they move into the parents' home, their lives will be restricted because they will have to look after him; but if they allow him to go into a Local Authority home, the money Brian is due to inherit on Roger's death will gradually reduce. It is of course possible that Roger's health will make it necessary for him to go into a National Health Service Hospital rather than a Local Authority home, in which case the money will remain intact; there is no charge for care by the National Health Service. It might not be surprising if, when the time comes for a decision to be made about Roger's future, Brian prefers that he should go into hospital. It is not a decision, however, that Brian will make; it is a matter to be decided by the Health Authorities, who will rely on the views of the family doctor and will make their own assessment of Roger's condition and his needs.

In the case of Alice Baker, the Court of Protection had a similar role to play, but the family circumstances were different. Alice's grandfather had directed in his will that a quarter of his estate should be held in trust for her. His solicitor had not known, when preparing the will, that Alice was mentally handicapped, so he gave no warnings about the effect that this might have on Alice's existing income. She was at an Adult Training Centre and received the full Supplementary Benefit which was extremely useful to her parents, as her father had retired early. As soon as Alice became entitled to her share of her grandfather's money, her entitlement to Supplementary Benefit ceased. Two applications had to be made by her father: one to the Department of Health and Social Security, so that she might transfer to the Non-Contributory Invalidity Pension; the other to the Court of Protection, so that her property could be managed on her behalf. This was extremely distressing so far as her parents were concerned: the amount of extra income from her newly-acquired property was not enough to make up for the difference between the Invalidity Pension and the lost Supplementary Benefit. The fees charged by the Court would have reduced this income even further, but the Court decided to postpone payment of these fees. It has power to do this when hardship can be caused to the handicapped person, or to the family. In spite of this, Alice's parents wished that they could have explained to her grandfather that the will made things worse for them, not better. It was, of course, too late.

WILLS

Everyone who owns property should make a will. Some people put off will-making for superstitious reasons; some say that everything will go to their relations anyway, so why bother? This is not at all sensible, partly because it is more troublesome to deal with the estate of someone who has not made a will, and partly because the rules of 'Intestate Succession' do not always work as people expect. Handicapped people who own property should of course make a will. We have just seen that the Court of Protection made a will for Roger White. The Court has power to make wills for those who are unable to do it for themselves, and it can prepare a will in accordance with what are most likely to be the wishes of the handicapped person.

A testator, the person who makes the will, must understand what he is doing, and there are various formalities described in this book. We are concerned here with wills made by

handicapped people, not wills under which they are beneficiaries. Many of them are fully competent to declare their
wishes in a will. For example, a person suffering from spasticity
may be unable to sign the document, but it can be signed for
him, in his presence, and at his direction, after he has indicated
what he wants. A will completed in this way will be perfectly
valid.

Some people who are mildly handicapped may be able to
make a will. They can do this, if they understand that they, like
everyone else, will die one day, and if they can express a wish as
to what is to happen to their money, their belongings, and any
other property they know they own. The will of a mentally
handicapped person should be witnessed by a doctor, and
certainly prepared by a solicitor, to ensure that there is no
likelihood of the will being disputed at a later date. One
possibility is that undue influence could be brought on a
mentally handicapped person, to persuade him to donate his
property to someone else. This is another reason for asking a
solicitor to prepare the will, and a doctor to witness it.

LIFE INSURANCE

A normal way of providing for one's relatives, or to cover the
liability involved in mortgaging one's house, is to take out a life
insurance policy. Handicapped people may not have dependent
relatives, but it is often desirable for their lives to be insured, if
only to provide enough money for a suitable funeral. It is of
course possible that the rates for insuring the life of a physically
handicapped person will be considerably higher than normal
rates, and this may also apply, to a lesser extent, to mentally
handicapped people.

Special rates have been negotiated for mentally handicapped
people with the Crusader Insurance Company Limited. To give
an example, at the time of publication it is possible to insure the
life of a mentally handicapped child under the age of 28 for
£500, paying 20 annual premiums of £16.53. This is sufficient
today to pay for a normal funeral. The cost is about 32p per

week; if the handicapped person is aged 45, the cost rises to 47p per week.

DEEDS OF COVENANT

If a parent or grandparent is not claiming tax relief in respect of a mentally handicapped child, then it may be possible for him to sign a deed of covenant, the effect of which would be to provide income for the benefit of the child. The covenant can be made in favour of the person who is caring for the child, e.g. by a grandparent in favour of the parent. The 'covenantor', i.e. the person signing the covenant, can deduct tax from the payments, and a claim for repayment of this tax can be made. The deed of covenant will not necessarily be in favour of the handicapped child, but of someone who will spend the money on his behalf.

SAVINGS

Parents quite often put money on one side for a handicapped person, in a Post Office Savings Account or a building society. If he is mentally handicapped, this money should be in the name of the parent or some other relative, partly to avoid the need for an application to the Court of Protection, and partly because of difficulties that may be raised by the Post Office or the building society if a signature is needed for the withdrawal of the money.

Other problems may result from savings in the name of a handicapped person, particularly if he has left no will. Gillian Browne gradually saved money for her handicapped son, putting the money into National Savings Certificates, Premium Bonds and a Post Office Savings Account. Her intention was to give him a small amount of money to spend on holidays and clothes. Her marriage broke up, and she had to manage on her own. Her son died in an accident, which was to some extent caused by his handicap. He had left no will, and all the money in his name, including the Savings Certificates and Premium Bonds, was divided between Mrs Browne and her former husband, they being his mother and father. Mrs Browne felt very bitter that her own efforts to save, and to teach her son to manage things for himself, should bring a benefit to the man who had deserted them. If she had left the money in her own name, or if her son had been able to make a will, this would not have happened.

GUARDIANSHIP

Guardians have been appointed to look after children from earliest times. Roman Law contains many instances of arrangements for guardianship. In our law, a guardian can now only be appointed, with very few exceptions, if a person is a minor, that is, under the age of eighteen. Until that age, his parents or his guardian, if one has been appointed, can take various decisions on behalf of the child, depending on his age.

Until recently, it was possible to appoint a guardian for most mentally handicapped people, but by the Mental Health Act 1983 this was changed. Today, a guardian can only be appointed for an adult if he or she suffers from 'mental disorder', which includes 'significant impairment of intelligence and social functioning *and* is associated with abnormally aggressive or seriously irresponsible conduct.' There are very few people in this category, which certainly does not include the great majority of those who are mentally handicapped.

So the situation today is that a guardian cannot normally be appointed for a mentally handicapped person. The parent of a handicapped person who is aged over eighteen is not his legal guardian. If their child is under eighteen years, a husband and wife have an equal right to appoint a guardian. They often include a clause in their wills, naming a particular person to carry out this task. This is a wise precaution, in case they should both die in an accident. It is of course essential to discuss the matter with the proposed guardian, to make sure that he or she is willing to assume the responsibility involved.

If parents are separated or divorced, each can appoint a guardian in their respective wills. If arguments arise between guardians, or between a guardian appointed by a deceased parent and the surviving parent, these have to be referred to a court to decide. The court has the power to remove a guardian, if it thinks this is right. Decisions are always made in the interests of the child, not of the parents or guardians.

8 A Place to Live

A problem faces our society: where are handicapped people to live when they survive their parents, or when their parents become too old to care for them? As we have seen, most handicapped people live at home with their families. It is also a fact that many of those who would, some years ago, have died before their parents, are now outliving them.

Government policy has resulted in the discharge of many people from hospitals, especially those who are mentally handicapped. In addition, Health Authorities are increasingly reluctant to admit mentally handicapped people to hospital, unless they need medical treatment. In 1974, there were 51,000 people in mental handicap hospitals and units. By 1977, this had dropped to 48,000, and in 1981 the figure was 43,000.

At the same time, the number of handicapped people living in residential homes is steadily growing. In 1969, there were 38,000 people in homes each of which contained less than 50 beds; this had grown to 61,000 in 1981. There was an overall increase in accommodation provided by Local Authorities in England and Wales from 82,000 in 1959 to 116,000 in 1970, and there has been a further increase since then. These figures include accommodation for those handicapped by old age, as well as other forms of handicap.

The number of handicapped people is tending to increase, probably because they are living longer. The cost to the public purse is large, and will almost certainly increase. To quote some more figures, the net current expenditure by Local Authorities in England in 1981-1982 on elderly people and on others with various forms of handicap was:

Elderly people, and younger people with physical handicap	£348,700,000
Mentally handicapped people	£ 65,100,000
Mentally ill people	£ 11,100,000

These figures are quoted to give an idea of the national scale of the problem. It is known that, in any given Local Authority Social Services area, there are likely to be about 80 mentally handicapped people, living with a parent or parents who are 75 years or older. Inevitably, these handicapped people will soon have to be cared for by someone else. Yet at the present time, Local Authorities are finding it very difficult to allocate funds to create residential homes.

There is of course great anxiety on the part of parents. In Chapter 4 there are notes of some real cases that have occurred in the recent past. Where, ask parents, will my child live when I die? The Local Authority may not be in a position to give any firm promise, and the majority of parents neither expect nor wish that other members of their family should take on the task of caring for their handicapped brother, sister or other relative.

Having cared for their handicapped child for forty years or more, many parents are most reluctant to see him transferred to a home or hostel. It has been a common experience in many parts of the country that the parents of handicapped children have told the Authorities, and the representatives of interested charities, that they very badly need residential accommodation for their child. Yet when the accommodation actually becomes available, those same parents often say that they are not ready for their child to leave home. The place held for him is given to someone else - perhaps from a hospital - and they are left in the same state of anxiety as before. There is a very good reason for parents' reluctance to let their child go: they know full well that even a good group home or hostel could not possibly give the same degree of care and attention that they have, for many years, given to their child. At the moment of decision, they find themselves unable to release him. In these circumstances, however, parents should consider whether they are really helping their child by keeping him with them, when he has the opportunity to go to a permanent home where they can see him settled for the rest of his life. It is possible that a difficult decision, taken today, will be of great benefit to him in the years to come.

Mrs Harris was in exactly this position. She had asked the Social Services Department to make a place in a home for her daughter, Suzanne, and, with other parents, had sent petitions to Councillors demanding that a suitable home should be built. After some years, a large house was acquired by the Council and turned into a hostel; Suzanne was offered a room of her own there, but Mrs Harris was not at all sure that she could bear to see her go. She asked herself whether Suzanne might be unhappy, whether she would find or make friends in the hostel, and whether she would be given the right food and personal care. At first, she refused to let Suzanne leave home, but it happened that one of Suzanne's friends from the Adult Training Centre was going to move into the hostel. Suzanne said she would like to go with her, and it proved possible to let them have a shared room, which they both wanted. This removed some, although not all, of Mrs Harris's doubts, and the two handicapped women moved into the hostel. Fortunately, the move was a great success, and Mrs Harris was happy to see her daughter finally settled.

Like some other parents, Mrs Harris was also anxious on financial grounds. On behalf of Suzanne, she had been collecting quite a large sum of money each week by way of Benefits and Allowances, and the loss of this income would make a major difference to her. Fortunately, she found that, when Suzanne left, she was able to move into a small flat on her own, where the expenses were far less. The flat was not far from the hostel, and Suzanne was able to come to see her mother regularly each week.

Matters do not always turn out so well as they did for Mrs Harris and her daughter. The young man, mentioned in

Chapter 4, who was put in a wholly unsuitable home intended for geriatric cases, had previously been offered a much more suitable place in a staffed hostel. His mother had been unable to make up her mind about the offer, and the Council had, in the end, given the place to someone else.

One problem facing parents is that they do not know what services are available generally, or in their own area. To make a sensible decision about their child's future, they must have this information. What are the likely alternatives?

Living with other members of their own family
Foster care
Independent living
Boarding out
Group homes
Hostels
National Health hospitals
Communities
The Mencap Homes Foundation

LIVING WITH THE FAMILY
When parents have become too old to care for their handicapped child, or have died, a very happy solution may be for him to live with a brother or sister, or some other close relative. This often happens, in which case there is no need for a search to be made for other accommodation. The majority of parents, however, react against the idea. They tend to feel that their other children have already had to put up with inconvenience, and perhaps with less attention during their childhood, by reason of the fact that their brother or sister is handicapped. It does not seem right to the parents that those children should also be expected to take on a further burden. Of course, there are many families where this is not the situation, and where a non-handicapped sister or brother is happy to continue to care for the handicapped sibling. In the majority of families, however, this is not what happens.

A common experience is that, while a brother may be content to take his handicapped sibling into his own home, this does not suit his spouse. Parents recognise this, and are often reluctant to bring pressure on their non-handicapped children to take a brother or sister in to live with them, even though this might be to their financial advantage.

FOSTER CARE

We have already seen that it is the legal duty of a Local Authority to make provision for handicapped people who are homeless, or threatened with homelessness. Accommodation in a Local Authority home or hostel can be expensive, costing (at current rates) upwards of £130 a week. A much less costly alternative is fostering. This approach has been used with success in the Leeds area, and also in other parts of the country. The Local Authority advertises in the press that it will make regular payments to any family willing to take a handicapped person into their home, and to treat him as a member of the family. The payment offered is about half the cost of keeping the person in a Local Authority home, but the fostering family have the additional advantage that the handicapped person will also receive Supplementary Benefit and other Allowances, which will help to cover the cost of food and other items.

The scheme works well, and there are many handicapped people now living in good foster homes. The payments from the Local Authority are not so large that they bring in a substantial profit to the foster parents, but they certainly cover all necessary expenses and make a valuable contribution towards the running of the home. The great value of the scheme, of course, is that the handicapped person is living with a family and receiving family care and attention. He can go to the Adult Training Centre or to a leisure club, just as other handicapped people do. One disadvantage, however, is that the situation may not be permanent; the foster parents may decide to move away, or change their house for a smaller one. They may decide that it is no longer convenient to continue to foster one or more handicapped people. The fostered person therefore has no security, and it is always possible that he will have to move from one home to another, never feeling that he really 'belongs' anywhere. Most parents, although content with good foster care on a temporary basis, would prefer to see their child settled in a permanent home.

INDEPENDENT LIVING

Many parents smile sadly when it is suggested that their handicapped child might be able to live on his own, provided he has regular support and can instantly seek help in a crisis. It would be quite impossible, they say. For a great many handicapped people, independent living is out of the question. Experience has shown, however, that many of them have in fact been able to live on their own, or at least in a small flat or bedsitter, once they have grown out of the state of total dependence in which they have been living.

Maureen moved out of her own home when her mother became crippled with arthritis. She went to a large staffed hostel, where she was given a room of her own. Over a period of two years she was given the chance to help in the hostel, and became involved in cooking, cleaning and mending clothes, tasks that her mother had always done for her while she was at home. In the third year, the hostel staff thought that it would be safe to try an experiment: Maureen moved temporarily into a small independent flat attached to the hostel - it was in fact a portakabin which had been set up in the garden behind the house. She went there with another woman of her own age; they had separate rooms, but they were expected to manage everything for themselves. The hostel staff visited when invited, or when asked for help. Within months it was clear that Maureen could manage very well and had the sense to ask for help when she needed it. She then moved, with the other woman, into a nearby flat built by a housing association, and they are still living there independently. If ever they require help they can get it. Maureen's mother has visited her and is unhappy about the very untidy state of her room, but it is perfectly clear to her, and to everyone else, that her daughter is able to manage on her own.

BOARDING OUT

There are many boarding houses throughout the country. Most of the people living in them are staying only for a short time, perhaps while they complete a job of work nearby, or in the hope of finding a permanent home. Some boarding houses are popular with people taking a holiday by the seaside. In recent years, the difficulties of Local Authorities in providing somewhere for disabled, handicapped or old people to live have led them increasingly to pay boarding houses to take them in. This may suit the proprietors of the boarding houses quite well, especially at times of the year when business is slack. Some of them have found that they are able to make a good profit from this business.

Unfortunately, a boarding house is not a permanent home, nor is it normally suitable for a handicapped person. Often, the rules of the home require residents to leave the property after breakfast each day, and they may not be permitted to return until the early evening. The majority of such houses are well run, but there are some where the owners are really only interested in profit, not in the welfare of residents. Those who need some degree of care are totally unsuitable as residents, and there have been cases in which handicapped people have been roaming the streets of seaside towns, unable to return to the boarding house until evening, whatever the weather. Under the Health and Social Services and Social Security Adjudications Act 1983, however, it is now necessary for these places to be inspected and licensed. This will improve boarding-house standards to some extent, but it will never give handicapped people what they are entitled to - a home of their own. Parents will naturally want to ensure, if they can, that their own children do not have to go to boarding houses, and they should take steps to learn what arrangements are normally made by their own Local Authority.

GROUP HOMES

A group home is one where several handicapped people live together, sometimes with a room of their own, sometimes sharing. In most such homes, there are one or more staff there, with various tasks, according to the abilities of the residents. For example, one group home may have only one resident member of staff; at such a home, the handicapped people will be taking responsibility for most of the work done in keeping the place tidy and clean. If there are common rooms, for example a dining room and a sitting room, as well as bathrooms and toilets, there will be some system for the division of work, perhaps a rota or an allocation of tasks to different people. The staff member who 'lives in' may not even cook for the residents, but may be there only to deal with any problems, to manage the finances of the home, and to act as a representative of the owners, who will in all probability be the Local Authority, or possibly a housing association.

Group homes may of course be created by charities, and some are built by housing associations. The residents, who will often have a legal tenancy of their rooms, will be expected to pay rent, and also contribute to the costs of heating, lighting and cleaning. They will do this from their earnings, if they have work, or from Supplementary Benefits and other payments made to them. The salaries of the staff, however, will be covered by the Local Authority or other agency which has set up the home. In fact, the phrase 'group home' covers a great many different types of provision, where residents have varying degrees of dependence. Normally, there is a good deal of practical care and supervision offered by a qualified person, or by several, and the use of the word 'home' in the title is significant, in that it implies that the people who live there are likely to be staying on a permanent basis. From the point of view of most parents of handicapped children, this may be the best provision available; if they are fortunate enough to see their child settled in such a home, much anxiety will be relieved.

HOSTELS

Many handicapped people live permanently in hostels. To a visitor, some places designated as a 'hostel' may look very like a 'Group Home', and may function in much the same way. However, there is likely to be less active supervision of residents in a hostel, and there will probably be more people living there than in a group home. While it is not likely that there will be more than seven or eight residents of a home, there are many hostels with over twenty residents.

All hostels have staff, or at least non-handicapped people, in residence. There are some, for example, where handicapped people and students live in roughly equal numbers. Such hostels exist in Cardiff and Norwich. The students take on a generally supportive role and help handicapped residents with tasks they cannot manage. Necessarily, they tend to stay for only three years or so, while the handicapped people are much more likely to live there for many years. In more than one home, the handicapped residents regard the students with slight – though friendly – condescension, treating them good-humouredly as 'birds of passage'. The arrangement is normally satisfactory to both groups, who derive support from one another.

Most hostels do not have students and handicapped people sharing, but are more likely to be provided for a group who all have the same, or a similar, handicap. Some are described as 'half-way houses', where people live who have suffered from mental illness, or perhaps from alcoholism, or who are returning to society after a period in prison. These groups are not, of course, mixed with one another, but the people within them live together, with a greater or lesser degree of supervision and support, depending on their need.

Hostels are usually in fairly large older houses. Like group homes, most of them are provided by Local Authorities under their statutory powers contained in Part III of the National Assistance Act 1948, as supplemented by the Housing (Homeless Persons) Act 1977, and other legislation.

NATIONAL HEALTH HOSPITALS

As we have already seen, there was a time when the majority of mentally handicapped people, and many others, were placed in mental handicap hospitals. These still exist, and they vary considerably in size and in the quality of life of those who live there. Because of the Government policy of placing mentally handicapped people in homes in the community rather than in large institutions, the number of those living in mental handicap hospitals dropped by more than 15% between 1974 and 1981. The aim of this policy is that the day will come when only those who need the medical care that hospitals provide are having to live in them; it is intended that all others shall live in various types of homes and hostels.

It is important to see the truth in relation to these hospitals. The great majority of their staff are caring people, although many of them are expected to do so much work that they have little if any time to provide personal care for their charges. In a few hospitals, unfortunately, there are people who act cruelly and without concern for the residents. It is these people who have caused some of the scandals that have been so well publicised in the popular press, and on radio and television, in recent years. Stories of brutal and inhuman treatment, and of patients being treated like animals, have occasionally been found to have some truth in them. Others have been shown to be false, or grossly exaggerated. Nothing less than a constant independent system of monitoring, and the allocation of sufficient public money to ensure proper staff levels, will satisfy those people and organisations who rightly criticise some - not all - of these places.

Many of the smaller hospitals, in particular, are known to give a good and caring service, and even in the larger ones there are many instances of constructive activities and a worthwhile life for residents. Observers tell of dedicated staff, usually underpaid and always over-worked, trying to preserve human dignity and happiness in very difficult circumstances. Occasionally, though, standards have broken down, and there are mental handicap hospitals where conditions are primitive, sometimes unpleasant. Some parents, having visited such places, are appalled at the mere thought that their own child might have to go there.

It is impossible to generalise about hospital provision without doing an injustice to staff on the one hand, or papering over the cracks on the other. Certainly it is the view of the majority of parents, and of professionals in the field of social welfare, that those who are handicapped should only be in a hospital if their physical or mental condition demands it. Unfortunately, as public funds are short, there are still many people who, instead of going into a suitable group home or hostel, are put in a mental handicap hospital. This also happens to physically handicapped people, and to those who suffer from spasticity.

COMMUNITIES

Because of the shortage of accommodation in places supported or financed by the State or by Local Government, there are a few privately-run homes, catering for people whose families are able to afford to pay fees. At the time of writing, these tend to range between £150 and £200 a week, and it therefore takes a substantial amount of private capital to ensure that someone will remain in them permanently. In addition to private provision, various charities have set up homes and villages of their own. The main such homes are run by:

The Home Farm Trust

This trust was set up in 1962 by a group of parents of mentally handicapped children who could see no prospect that their own children would be able to move into a good home after leaving school at age 16. After 21 years, the trust had created nine homes, in Gloucestershire, Yorkshire, Warwickshire, Cheshire,

Devon, Kent, Oxfordshire and Hertfordshire, with a present overall total of more than 200 residents. Several homes have more than thirty residents, and it is a policy of the trust to have people with varying degrees of handicap in each home.

It is not surprising that the Home Farm Trust began to receive more applications than it had places. There was no alternative but to set up a waiting list, which at present has around 1,000 names. In recent years, new places have been created at a rate of about 60 a year, and there is therefore a constant need for fund-raising on a national basis, with groups coming together in all parts of the country to gather in the necessary funds. Each home costs over £500,000 to buy, repair and equip. Parents who have put their children on the waiting list are of course invited to make donations to the trust, during their lives by gift or by deed of covenant, or in their wills by legacy. As with any charity, the trust cannot make donations a condition of acceptance of a particular handicapped person, nor will it guarantee a place for him, however large the property that parents may transfer to the trust. See Appendix II for an explanation of the law on this subject.

Residents are selected by the trust on the basis of need and of suitability for a particular home, and a high place on the waiting list does not automatically entitle them to be given a home. Nevertheless, the higher up the list, the better the chance that a place will be found for them. The address of the Home Farm Trust is 43 Queens Road, Bristol.

CARE

Those who set up CARE, in 1966, aimed to establish a series of village communities where mentally handicapped men and women, over the age of 18, could live and work as normally as possible. The first village was established near Tiverton, in Devon, and there are now other villages in Leicestershire, Lancashire, West Sussex, Kent and Newcastle-upon-Tyne. In all, there are more than 200 villagers, and the staff who work with and care for them number at least 100.

Each CARE village has a group of cottages and houses, with work areas, a 'village hall', and accommodation for staff. A typical modern village house will have seven bed-sitting rooms for people with mental handicap, and a two-room flat for the house-parent. There are bathrooms and toilets, and a kitchen. Meals are taken in a large room where there are tables, but also easy chairs, television and a gramophone. The residents can have privacy in their own rooms, but they can live a communal life if they prefer. The mid-day meal is taken in the village hall where there are large areas for tables and chairs, and a kitchen. The workshops are given over to woodwork, carpet- and doll-making, and other activities. The village in Leicestershire is particularly proud of its printing press, which produces the Christmas cards that CARE sells every year to support its general work.

Residents have a choice of where they work, but they are expected to take up some kind of employment. This may be in the kitchen, in the gardens, in the vegetable plot or in the workshops. The atmosphere is cheerful and relaxed, and for many parents it will be the ideal setting for their handicapped child, especially if they would prefer him to live in a small house or cottage, rather than in the big buildings that the Home Farm Trust have acquired for their residents. There is no doubt that those handicapped people who live in the villages live a life that is for the most part separate from the rest of the community, but this may suit them and their parents perfectly well. As would be expected, the CARE villages have a waiting list which has more names than the actual number of residents now in the villages. Because of this, efforts continue to raise money and to buy new land on which villages can be built. This is a very costly undertaking and involves a considerable amount of effort, especially on the part of parents who hope that their child may perhaps be able to move into a village at some time in the future.

CARE insist, as do the Home Farm Trust, that all residents shall be sponsored by a Local Authority which is expected to pay (at the time of writing) about £130 a week for each individual. The selection of residents is concerned with the ability of the individual to fit into, enjoy and contribute to the village community. Villages have both men and women, although in the cottages and houses they are usually grouped together, the men living upstairs and the women downstairs.

It is probably true to say that the majority of parents would prefer to see their child settled in the protective environment of a Home Farm Trust home, or a CARE village, than in an ordinary house in an ordinary road. Fortunately, there is no need for those who advocate a less protected style of life to argue with others who take a different view. The need for places is so great that there is ample room for organisations with differing philosophies.

THE MENCAP HOMES FOUNDATION

The National Association for Backward Children was set up in 1955. Its main task was to fight for mentally handicapped children to have the same rights as other people, and it drew its strength from over 400 local societies in all parts of England, Wales and Northern Ireland. It changed its name to the National Society for Mentally Handicapped Children, and later added the words 'and Adults' to this title. People with mental handicap were living much longer than expected, and were growing to adulthood. Successful pressure was mounted to ensure that they received an education, and a growing number of community homes were created by the Statutory Authorities. In 1982, Mencap, as it became known, was allowed to take on the title of the Royal Society.

By that time, most of the necessary legislative changes had been made that parents had demanded, but the shortage of Government money meant that far too few suitable community homes had been created. Members of local societies began to write to Mencap, offering to give their homes to the Royal Society if it would take on the responsibility of looking after their children. In response to this need, expressed by its own members, Mencap decided to take action. It created the Homes Foundation, an organisation within the Royal Society whose aim was, and is, to provide permanent homes for mentally handicapped adults.

If provision by the Health and Local Authorities had been sufficient, it would not have been necessary to set up the Foundation, for it was generally agreed that the provision of homes was really the responsibility of the Statutory Authorities. There were some objections within Mencap on this score, but as time went by it became clear that unless the Royal Society took action, as other charities were doing, many handicapped people would be without a proper home when their parents died.

In contrast with other charities, Mencap decided that it would try to provide ordinary homes in the community, rather than create large communities in country houses, or set up special villages. This implied no criticism of the other charities, but is seen as a valid alternative approach. Where, though, could the houses be found? One could not expect a group of parents to die at more or less the same time, all in the same area, leaving their houses (and the children) in Mencap's care. It was decided to seek homes, or the money to build them, from these sources:

- Houses given by parents and relatives of mentally handicapped people.
- Cash and other property similarly donated.
- National charities with a special interest in people with handicap.
- Local Authority housing accommodation.
- Housing associations, whose money could be obtained from the Housing Corporation.
- Joint funding, an arrangement under which National Health Service money is made available to Local Authorities and to voluntary organisations.

When considering the possibility of receiving donations

from parents and relatives, Mencap struck its first difficulty: a court case decided in 1926 (of which details are given in Appendix II) made it impossible for a charity to enter into a legal bargain with parents to provide a home for their child in return for the transfer of their house, even if this was done by will. The Royal Society had already met a similar problem in creating its Trustee Visitors Service (see page 88), and it solved it in the same way: although it was under no legally binding obligation to provide a home for a child whose parents had given their house, it could nonetheless decide to do this - as part of its general charitable work - without being forced to do so. If several handicapped people could be shown to be living in a house, and not only the child of the parents who had given it, Mencap's action could be shown to be legally charitable, and not a bargain with one particular family.

This in fact happened in the case of a young man whom we shall call Jack Heath. Jack's father made his will some years before the Homes Foundation was created, but he gave all his money to Mencap. The Royal Society could have devoted the money, and the house which Mr Heath also gave, to its general work, but it decided instead to try to find some way, within the Homes Foundation plan, to use the sale money to provide a home for Jack. The house had to be sold, because it was not big enough to use as a home for several handicapped people, with room also for a house parent. It took a long time to get the scheme under way: in the first place, the executor of Mr Heath's property took many months to sell the house; then it was necessary to start negotiations with the Local Authorities. This was essential because, although the Homes Foundation's aim is to provide homes, it cannot also take on responsibility for everyday running costs. If the money given to Mencap were to be used up in that way, it would be exhausted in a few years and the hopes of parents would be frustrated. Negotiations, therefore, had to be undertaken with the Social Services Department of the County Council. Fortunately, they were extremely co-operative. Not only did they want to see a home provided for Jack (who was temporarily living in a hospital), but they had several other handicapped people for whom they wanted to find a home.

At this stage, the Homes Foundation brought in the local Mencap Society, and also the Health Authority. It was obvious that no national organisation could run homes all over the country from its London headquarters; local people would have to be involved in the preparation of a plan. One obvious source for recruiting volunteers for this work was within the local Mencap Society which represented parents, many of whom had known Mr Heath. The Health Authority would also prove a good ally, partly because it had responsibility for the health of residents in any home that could be created, but also because it was keen that Jack should be moved out of hospital, and into a home in the community.

It was clearly necessary to find or build a place which would take about six handicapped people, thus justifying the salary of someone who could care for them all. The local Housing Authority in the place where Jack had lived was a District Council, not the County Council. They were asked to join the partnership made up of the County Social Services Department, the Health Authority, the Royal Society and the local Mencap Society, and they agreed to provide a pair of cottages. These were in very bad repair, but structurally sound, and the Homes Foundation, knowing that it would soon be receiving the money from the sale of Mr Heath's home, agreed to have the houses repaired, adapted for use by handicapped people, and furnished. Special provision was made for Jack, who used a wheelchair, to live in a downstairs room, and five other people were selected to move in with him.

This arrangement broke no law relating to charities, nor did it create a legal trust for Jack's benefit. Mencap was under no legal obligation to provide him with a home, but was certainly not prevented from doing so. What was more, by using Jack's father's money as it did, in co-operation with others, it fulfilled its task of giving help to mentally handicapped people generally. Local parents, who had been rather doubtful whether they could transfer their houses to the Homes Foundation without any guarantee, saw that the result of Mr Heath's gift was in fact a good home for his son, and decided to change their wills so that the Homes Foundation could benefit.

The Homes Foundation decided at an early stage that it would be absolutely essential for all parents deciding to give property to the Foundation, in the hope that their child would be found a home, to be independently and separately advised by their own solicitor. The dangers of any other course were obvious: if Mencap itself helped people to prepare wills under which its Homes Foundation was to receive property, the charge could one day be made that it had influenced the parents in an unfair way, and the wills might be altered by a decision of a court. Mencap, as do many charities, has a great deal of experience of dealing with wills disputed by disgruntled relatives. It did not want to find itself in this situation by reason of gifts to the Homes Foundation. The best way to provide against this was to insist that parents approached their own solicitors. However, for the guidance of solicitors, some draft clauses for wills have been prepared, and these are set out in Appendix I.

At an early stage of development of the Homes Foundation, Mencap was approached by another large national charity whose representatives asked what projects were currently in hand. They were especially interested in the Homes Foundation, then only a project, and they decided to make a large donation, to enable a house to be bought in whatever part of the country Mencap might select. It so happened that the Homes Foundation plan had been printed and distributed to all Social Services Departments and all Health Authorities, as well as to local Mencap Societies. There was general approval, but one particular Social Services Department expressed great interest, and added that it would be happy to co-operate with Mencap in developing a Homes Foundation home in its area. It was obvious that this would be a suitable place for the charity's money to be used, and a search was made in the county town for a house. Mencap's own regional staff became closely involved.

One local Mencap Society, at Halesowen, had already set up a very satisfactory home, and the new Homes Foundation development was modelled to some extent on this. At Halesowen, the local Mencap Society had collected a large sum of money and had erected, on land owned by the Local Council, a building large enough to house fourteen mentally handicapped people. Each resident had his or her own room, but there were two large sitting rooms, a big kitchen and a large, bright dining room. After two years of running the house, it became clear that three of the ladies living there were becoming more and more competent. It was obvious that they could live together in a house of their own, if suitable arrangements could be made. The adjoining property was also owned by the Local Council, and a council house had just become vacant. After some discussions, it was agreed that the three handicapped ladies should move in there. They were already friends, but the parents of one had misgivings about the move. In fact, the new arrangement worked extremely well. If ever there was a difficulty they could not solve, they had only to walk across to the main house where staff lived who could give immediate help.

In the following year, it became possible to move three men into another council house, although it was decided this time that they would probably need more help from staff in the main building, and a small wicket-gate was put in the fence between the two properties. The men who are now living there still take some of their meals in the main building, but otherwise they live their own lives. Every time residents moved out of the central house – known as the 'core' of the unit – there was room for more handicapped people to move in. The Social Services Department at Halesowen found that it was far less expensive for them to sponsor people to live in that house than in one of their own homes, so they sent more people there. After several years, there had built up a 'cluster' of several small houses and flats, the residents depending when necessary on the staff in the 'core' unit, but otherwise living independently.

At the Homes Foundation house which had been bought with money from the charity, it was agreed to create a 'core and cluster' group of houses. Severely handicapped people were to live in the main house, with staff always available to care for them. In the surrounding homes, less handicapped people moved in. The County Council's Social Services Department set up a Social Training Unit within walking distance of the home, and the residents were able to go there, to learn to manage better for themselves. The cluster of surrounding homes were bought, using money from the Government-financed Housing Corporation which was allocated to the New Era Housing Association, an association linked closely with Mencap.

This group of homes, bought with money from the charity and from the Housing Corporation, had to be properly managed. It was agreed that a management committee, consisting of representatives from the County Social Services Department, the Health Authority, the local Mencap Society and Mencap's Regional Office, should take on responsibility for appointing staff and generally supervising the operation of the project. The committee accepted financial responsibility, not only for repairs, payment of staff and normal running expenses, but also for regular payments to the Housing Corporation of interest on the money it had provided. Payments by, or on behalf of, individual residents had also to be organised. Each of them was able to contribute income, either from earnings or - more likely - from Supplementary Benefits and other Allowances. This had to be collected by staff and paid into a bank account in the name of the Homes Foundation. Salaries and most bills were paid out of this account, which was managed by the Head Office of the Homes Foundation, at Mencap's Headquarters. The amount of money paid by residents did not meet all the expenses, so the Social Services Department, which remained enthusiastic about the project, made up the balance.

In other parts of the country, the Homes Foundation was developing two homes, each of which had been bought by the New Era Housing Association. The residents were relatively mildly handicapped, and only a few staff were required to live in. Again, local management committees were formed, with representation from Health and from Social Services. The aging parents of children who would soon need separate accommodation were persuaded – with some reluctance – to allow their children to move into the homes which are now operating successfully. In the case of each home, the Local Council provided sufficient money to 'top-up' the cost of running the place; this was much less expensive for the Councils than it would have been to keep handicapped people in homes they had built.

One of the great advantages of the Homes Foundation is therefore that it saves ratepayers' money. The reason is that the Local Council does not have to provide capital. Other homes (for old people and others who are entitled to accommodation under Part III of the National Assistance Act 1948) have to be built with borrowed money. Councils must pay high interest charges on this money, and this increases the cost of providing each person with a home. When this money is found by a charity, from its own or from parents' resources, or from the Housing Corporation, the cost to the ratepayer is greatly reduced. This gives Local Councils a considerable incentive to co-operate with voluntary and charitable organisations.

As time goes on, and as more Homes Foundation homes are created, so more and more parents will find themselves willing to take part in the scheme and give their own homes to the Foundation, in the hope that room will be found for their own children and for other mentally handicapped people, when the time comes. It is not easy for parents to take this step, because of the uncertainties about where their child will live, and who will be his companions. Ideally, parents would like their child to continue to live in his own home, preferably in his own bedroom, cared for by one person who will do everything that they have done. This is normally not practicable. One difficulty is that so few modern houses are really suitable. A home has to accommodate five or six people, for it is only on this basis that the Local Authority is likely to be able to finance staff salaries and other expenses. The majority of private homes cannot offer room for so many. The likelihood is therefore that some houses bequeathed to the Homes Foundation will have to be sold, as Mr Heath's was, and the money used to adapt, improve or build new accommodation.

A very real difficulty for the Homes Foundation is the selection of residents. It is clear that this is best done by professionals, although there also has to be parent representation. A typical selection committee will therefore have members from the local Mencap Society, but also from the Social Services and Health Authorities. It is important to see that justice is done, and that selection is impartial. If it were left entirely to representatives of the local Mencap Society and the Homes Foundation, the basis of selection might well be criticised.

Some parents have gained the impression that the Homes Foundation is designed only for mentally handicapped people whose parents own a home or have a lot of money. This is not so. The first Homes Foundation unit, opened in London in 1982, was given to Mencap by a charity associated with a large hospital. None of the nine residents there made any kind of contribution to the cost of buying or equipping the home. The same is true of the residents of the great majority of other Homes Foundation units. Fortunately, no parent of a mentally handicapped child has ever objected to the fact that other handicapped people will benefit from a gift he is making, although of course he also hopes that the Homes Foundation will look after his own child.

What can a parent do if he has no home and no money resources, but would like to see a Homes Foundation home created in his area, which could provide accommodation for his child, now or in the future? He should recruit other like-minded parents in the area, and together with them should explore, with the Homes Foundation staff at its Headquarters, ways in which public money can be made available to buy, build or create the first homes. Often, the Housing Department of the Local Authority may be willing to allow the Homes Foundation to take over an older building, especially if it can find the money – through an Urban Aid Grant, through Joint Funding, through a Housing Association or by other means – to make the necessary alterations. Having set up the scheme, it is quite possible that other parents will join who do have property they can donate, by their wills.

There will inevitably be times when a particular resident of a Homes Foundation home will have to move to other accommodation. This may be a move to greater independence, or it may be necessary because of the deterioration of his condition. In any event, the Homes Foundation has decided that, having taken on responsibility for an individual, it will continue to be responsible for his care on a permanent basis.

The Homes Foundation is still in its early stages of development, but it is already proving successful. The Royal Society expects that local Mencap Societies, some of which are already running homes of their own, will bring them within the scope of the Homes Foundation, so that national support is available, and also continuity of management. At the same time, there is no reason why other groups should not develop schemes similar to that of the Foundation. The need is great, and is growing all the time. Every year that passes brings more parents to an age when they can no longer look after their adult handicapped child; they have every possible incentive to see him happily settled in a satisfactory home managed by an organisation which has their confidence.

SAVINGS SCHEMES
Some parents understandably want their non-handicapped children to receive a share of their property. They often say that they consider that the other children have already had to suffer

by reason of having a handicapped brother or sister, and do not want them to do without any benefit under their wills. One way of achieving this is to set up a savings scheme to add to the amount of property that will eventually be available for division. Such a scheme is explained in the next chapter.

As has been said before in this book, too late can mean too little. If the parents of a young handicapped child begin to make modest savings at an early stage of his life, this will very likely result in a large fund being available. This greatly increases the options open to them. In contrast to older generations, many young parents now feel that, having looked after their handicapped child for twenty years or so, he or she should then have the chance of a more independent life, as do other children. If the parents have, over those years, built up a sum of money through a savings scheme, this may give them the chance to contribute to the Homes Foundation, or other charitable projects, and see their child settled at a time when they are themselves still in their middle years.

Many families with a handicapped child find that it is impossible for both husband and wife to work, so great is the practical burden of care that they have to carry. This may mean that, even taking Allowances into account, it is impossible to make savings for the child's future. Parents in this situation need not despair, nor resign themselves to a lifetime of anxiety. While they still have the will and the capacity, they should work with other parents to see that enough residential provision is made in their own area. They could approach the Homes Foundation or one of the other charities mentioned earlier in this chapter, or they could even create a local charity themselves. They could work with a local housing association, or with the New Era Housing Association, to create local homes. They will find that there will be many local groups and associations who will be glad to help them; it is always easier to raise money for the bricks and mortar of a home than it is for the general purposes of a charity.

9 Options – and Solutions

Parents of a handicapped child have far more options than they realise. If they act early enough they can make a real difference to the life he will live. Even if they have reached retirement age, and have not made any definite plans, it is still not too late to take some action. This chapter summarises the options that parents have, and the action they can take, by posing a series of questions. At the end of the chapter there is an analysis of a flexible plan which can be adopted – or adapted – by parents, so as to make provision for their whole family, including their handicapped child.

Has your child been regularly assessed?
This is vital, from the earliest years. As soon as it appears that a child may be in some way handicapped, an assessment should be made. (See Chapter 4.) This enables all concerned, parents and professionals, to decide what educational programme ought to be developed for him. As the years go by, assessments should be renewed. Education may help him slowly to develop new skills; his condition may improve, or perhaps it will deteriorate. Either way, a change may be needed to his environment, his treatment, or his education. Assessment of his handicap will point the way that this change should take.

Is he receiving the right education?
Parents are legally entitled to know the result of an assessment, and to be consulted on the best education and training programme to suit their child. They are entitled to their say as to the school in which he is to be taught. For his benefit and theirs, these are rights that they should exercise. If there are

difficulties, or if the Authorities do not seem to be co-operative, they should seek advice. (See Chapter 5.)

Does your child have the opportunity to receive social education?
In some areas, there are social education centres, and in some, the work of the Health Visitor may include helping parents to teach basic social skills to their children. Sometimes, an Adult Training Centre, or a hostel, may have the facility to help a handicapped person to live more independently, possibly in a model flat annexed to the main building. If these opportunities exist, parents can press for their child to benefit from them. (See Chapter 2.)

Will your child stay on at school till age 19, and then continue to receive further education?
He is entitled to stay at school until his nineteenth birthday. Is it desirable that he should? How will he benefit from, say, two extra years at school? Could he - should he - start training for some sort of work, or is this out of the question? In the long term, what is best for him? Handicapped people are just as much entitled to further education as they are to primary and secondary education. If your child's handicap is such that he could benefit from some form of further education, every opportunity should be seized to make sure that he receives it. As with a non-handicapped child, further education may make all the difference to his future life. For example, there are several solicitors in practice today who suffer from spasticity; they took their examinations after a long period of study (as do all solicitors), served articles, and eventually qualified. Passing the examinations was not easy, because they needed help at many stages. Working in everyday practice is no easier, for some of them have to move about in wheelchairs. Yet they have surmounted all these problems. So can other handicapped people, in different ways, and at different levels of education. The key lies in their being given every possible opportunity to

continue with their education for as long as they can benefit from it.

Is there at least a chance that your child will be able to hold a job?

Many parents will read no further after seeing this question. But consider Janice, who was recruited into Mencap's Pathway Scheme. No one thought she was bright enough to do any kind of work; at an Adult Training Centre each day, she fitted small pieces of plastic together, and was paid pocket money of £4 a week. She worked reliably, and the manager of the Centre thought that perhaps she could do more. With many doubts, her parents allowed her to leave the Centre and go to work in a fruit-bottling factory. They were worried lest she might not get her place back at the Adult Training Centre, if she failed at the factory. They were also concerned because they relied on the Supplementary Benefit which Janice brought into the house each week. After six months, Janice had proved how wrong everyone's doubts had been. She enjoyed her new work very much; she was earning the standard rate of pay for the job. Her employer asked if there were any more like her.

'Never', he said, 'have I had a girl like Janice. She's very friendly, always gets in on time, never leaves early, never takes days off. She enjoys the job, even though it is repetitive. If I ask her to do something new or different, she learns it quite quickly, and if she has finished she comes to ask for more work!'

Handicapped people are often far more capable of doing a job than their friends and relatives think. Every chance should be taken to see that they do so, not only because it will be productive and rewarding, but also because it will introduce them to new people, and help them to live as normal a life as possible.

Is your child receiving every Benefit, Allowance and Pension to which he is entitled?

Check carefully through the Benefits detailed in Chapter 3, to see if you are claiming all that you can. It is your child's right to receive these Benefits, and he should be getting them *now*. If the day comes when you are no longer available to care for him, he will need them just as much as, if not more than he does now. If he is not already receiving them, it may take a long time for someone else to establish his right to them.

Is all necessary equipment available to help your handicapped child?
Not only are wheelchairs available, but also other aids. As we have seen in Chapter 4, Local Authorities must make arrangements for adapting homes for the comfort, safety and convenience of handicapped people. If in doubt as to what a handicapped person's entitlements may be, obtain advice from the Citizens' Advice Bureaux, a specialist voluntary organisation or charity, or from a solicitor.

Does your child enjoy recreation, leisure activities, and holidays?
These are his right - see the Chronically Sick and Disabled Persons Act 1970, explained in Chapter 4. Some parents are quite naturally frightened that recreation and holidays may lead their child into some danger and the possibility of injury, even if there is full supervision. Without doubt, there is always some risk, but it is the same with non-handicapped children; they may be bruised on the playing field, may sprain an ankle or cut themselves, and although we do not want this to happen we would not try to stop them from playing a game on this account. We need to take the same attitude to our handicapped children. It is not a question of sending them into foolhardy danger, but of accepting that almost all enjoyable sports and games, and holidays too, involve a small degree of risk. Parents can insist that their child is properly supervised at all times, of course. If this happens, then there is every reason why they should enlarge their lives with leisure activities. If they do this as they are growing up, they will continue to be able to

participate in the years to come, whether or not they still have their parents with them.

The child whose parents never allow him to take any risk may one day feel left out, if he is living at a home or hostel where supervised games are encouraged. Joseph once fell while he was kicking a ball. He sprained his ankle, and was confined to a wheelchair for some weeks. Joseph enjoyed being pushed from place to place, and decided that he would stay in the wheelchair. Although his foot was cured, he made things very difficult for his family when they tried to get him to walk on his own. After a time, they accepted that he would always have to be wheeled around the neighbourhood when he went out of doors, although he seemed to have no trouble at all in walking from the dining room to the living room when he wanted to watch television. Eventually, Joseph was admitted to a hostel where he was miserable for many months, simply because he was without his wheelchair. He had no physical need of it, and so the staff at the hostel insisted that he did without it. He sulked, and moved only when absolutely necessary. He could be seen gazing out of the window at other residents playing together on the grass, but he refused to take part in their games.

Is your child healthy?
Health is not just an absence of illness. Has he regularly seen the dentist, and the optician? Does he need any kind of physiotherapy? Most important of all, is his diet right, and is he the correct weight for his height and age? Many handicapped children, especially those suffering from Down's Syndrome, can easily become overweight if they are allowed to eat too much. So can the rest of us, but in the case of a handicapped child, health is of even greater importance.

Have arrangements been made for your child's future home?
The whole of Chapter 8 is devoted to this vital subject. Without repeating everything that is said there, it is of course essential that everything is done to ensure, so far as is humanly possible,

that he will have somewhere to go, whether to a relative, a Local Authority home, a suitable hospital, a Homes Foundation home, or some other place. As we have seen in Chapter 2, if no action is taken at all by parents, there is a risk that their handicapped child (though by then an adult) may be sent to a totally unsuitable place, and may have to stay there because there is nothing better available.

Have you made the best financial arrangements, during your life and by your will?
Chapters 6 and 7 of this book deal fully with wills, trusts, and property matters. Chapter 8 describes the residential accommodation that may be available. We conclude this chapter with a plan which families may care to adopt, one which has been designed to provide not only for the handicapped member, but also for the others. It contains frequent references to schemes operated by the Royal Society for Mentally Handicapped Children & Adults (Mencap), simply because these are among the best available, but there is nothing in these schemes which could not be adopted by other charities and voluntary organisations. They could be adapted so as to benefit people with other forms of handicap, and there is every reason why they should be.

PROVIDING FOR THE WHOLE FAMILY
Throughout this book, we have looked at ways in which all parents, whether or not they have a house or other resources, can ensure a better life for their handicapped child. Many actions can be taken by those parents who do not own property. For those who do, we have seen that rules and regulations affecting Supplementary Benefits and residential accommodation have made it exceptionally difficult for them to make satisfactory arrangements.

There is a need for a plan which parents can follow, whether their resources are large or small, and whether or not they have non-handicapped children to whom they wish to give a share of their property when they die. Such a plan must not create any form of trust which would give rise to a charge by a Local Authority, nor deprive a handicapped person of benefits. It must therefore be flexible, and must leave the ownership of the family's assets with parents for as long as possible.

These assets fall into three main categories: a freehold or leasehold house or flat; money or investments; and physical objects, such as jewellery, furniture, a car, silver and so on. In families without a handicapped member, parents will often decide that everything they own shall be divided equally between their children on their death. Their wills can therefore be relatively simple. Those parents who have a handicapped child may find it convenient to leave some of the family property to their non-handicapped children, and to set aside, through a savings plan, a separate fund from which, in one of various ways, a handicapped child may be able to benefit. The family's assets can be shown like this:

HOME (Freehold or Leasehold)
MONEY and **INVESTMENTS**
CAR, JEWELLERY, **FURNITURE, ETC.**
SAVINGS PLAN

Given a free choice, that is, leaving aside the statutory rules and regulations that affect handicapped people, the parents would like to be able to arrange their wills in the following way:

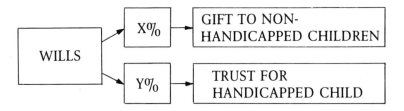

The symbols 'X%' and 'Y%' are used, as the actual proportions will depend on the number of children in the family. Ideally, parents would like to be able to create a trust which will give freedom to their trustees to allocate income, or if necessary capital, to their handicapped child, according to his need.

Those parents whose children are mentally handicapped can take part in the Mencap Trustee Visitors Service (see Chapter 4) and the Mencap Homes Foundation (see Chapter 8). They cannot be guaranteed a specific benefit for their child, because of the law relating to charities, but they know that his or her needs will be actively considered by Mencap. Having seen the way in which the Visitors Service and the Homes Foundation operate, they will know that it is not likely that their child will be excluded from benefit. They accept that, as a result of the donations they make, other mentally handicapped people will also benefit.

The missing element in the plan for a handicapped child is the provision of money for his everyday needs. So far as mentally handicapped children are concerned, the problem has now been solved through the use of a specially designed charitable fund, part of the Mencap City Foundation. The Foundation was created in 1982, and its initial funds were raised with the help of the then Lord Mayor of London, Sir Anthony Jolliffe. A Board of Governors, consisting of the parents of mentally handicapped children and of leading bankers, investment advisers and the directors of insurance companies, was appointed to administer the Foundation, and to make grants to aid projects in favour of mentally handicapped people. Much of the money paid into the fund was invested in the Mencap Unit Trust, which is managed by the M & G Company and was also created in 1982. Many investors in units are content to covenant their income to Mencap, and to take advantage of any increase in the capital value of their units. In the first year of operation, these units increased in value by 43%, but this is a rate of increase that could certainly not be expected to be maintained in later years.

A second function of the City Foundation is now the management of funds donated to it by parents or relatives of mentally handicapped people, or left to it by a legacy in their wills. Money thus given to the Foundation is carefully invested, sometimes in the Mencap Unit Trust, and the investments are managed on a regular basis. The income of the fund thus created can be made available to benefit any mentally handicapped person in the United Kingdom. No individual who is mentally handicapped has any right to income or capital from the fund, but the Foundation will certainly consider the interests of those children whose parents have made donations. The Foundation will of course also have to consider the needs of mentally handicapped people whose relatives have made no contributions; otherwise it might appear that it is operating some kind of secret trust, which would attract a charge from those Authorities providing residential accommodation; it would also deprive beneficiaries of their Supplementary Benefits.

If the parents of mentally handicapped children are willing to make donations to the Mencap Trustee Visitors Service and to the Homes Foundation, there is no reason why they should be unwilling to make similar gifts to the City Foundation. The plan would then operate as shown in the diagram opposite.

In order to help parents provide funds for the savings plan, Mencap devised a scheme, in 1984, under which the parents could make regular savings, and at the same time insure their lives. Thus, if they die earlier than expected, these savings, plus

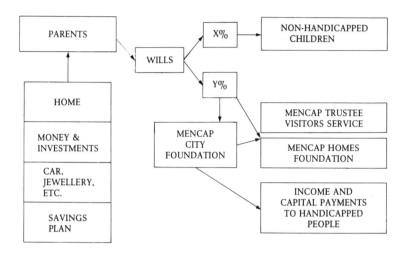

the life insurance policy money, can be paid to the City Foundation. If they live to normal retirement age, as most people do, there will be a substantial amount to be transferred to the Foundation. The cost of insuring one's life in this way is low, especially when it is spread over several years.

Parents will make their own decisions on the way in which they will allocate money, investments or other property to the City Foundation. They will complete a Family Form for the Foundation, just as they do for the Mencap Trustee Visitors Service and for the Homes Foundation. This Family Form concerns their child: it explains his likes and dislikes, the extent of his handicap, and the ways in which they think he could benefit from any money that the Foundation might decide to allocate to him. Money could be used, for example, for holidays and clothes; larger amounts might be needed for special equipment to help a handicapped person become mobile inside or outside his home, or for such items as a colour TV set, or a video-recorder.

As diagrams can be rather confusing, let us look at some examples. Mr and Mrs Weston have three children, all over the age of 18. The third child, Yvonne, is mentally handicapped and lives with her parents. She is 38 years old. The Westons own their home, have a little money in a building society, a valuable picture, a car, some jewellery and furniture. Mr Weston is living on a reasonable pension and has just inherited some money from an aunt who died recently, aged 92. He would like to find some way of providing a benefit for Yvonne. Mr and Mrs Weston visit their solicitor and, having been advised, they ask him to arrange their wills like this:

First, they want Yvonne to have a Visitor provided under the Mencap Trustee Visitors Service; the cost of this is to be a first charge on their property.

Second, they are reasonably certain that Yvonne will go to a local hostel when the time comes, so they are not interested in the Homes Foundation.

Third, they decide to give their house, with all its contents, equally to their two non-handicapped children.

Fourth, they would like to create a trust for Yvonne, but their solicitor advises that this would deprive her of Supplementary Benefit and lead to Local Authority charges being levied (see above), so they decide to set up a very small trust, for only £1,200, in her favour, to be administered by their executors. Their solicitor advises that this will prevent any challenge to the will under the Inheritance (Family Provision) legislation. (See Chapter 6.)

Fifth, they give the whole of the money bequeathed by Mr Weston's aunt, plus the sale value of the picture, to the Mencap City Foundation. They do this in the knowledge that, although Yvonne will have no legal entitlement to this money, nor to the income on it, the Trustees of the Fund will know of her needs and will bear them in mind when exercising their discretion. Mr and Mrs Weston realise that other mentally handicapped people may also benefit from this gift to the Foundation. With their will they will leave a detailed note concerning Yvonne, so that the Foundation will be fully informed about her. In addition, the Visitor appointed under the Mencap Trustee Visitors Service will keep an eye on Yvonne, and will report regularly on her needs.

Mr and Mrs Vernon are in a different situation. They have only one child, Alistair, who is handicapped and is now 15. They do not want to have any more children. They own their house, and they have life insurance policies which would pay off their mortgage if Mr Vernon were to die. They give these instructions to their solicitor:

First, they give a legacy, as the Westons did, to the Mencap Trustee Visitors Service, in the hope that Alistair will have a life-long Visitor. They realise that Mencap is not under a legal obligation to supply one, but they nominate Alistair to receive visits.

Second, they create a trust for £3,000 for Alistair, for the same reason as the Westons did.

Third, they give their home, on the death of the survivor of them, to the Homes Foundation, so that it can be used to provide accommodation for mentally handicapped people in their area. Mr Vernon is already taking steps to see that a Homes Foundation Group is formed, with other members of the local Mencap Society. The plan is to set up the first home with the help of the New Era Housing Association, but once this is occupied the administrative structure will be there to make use of the Vernons' present home, perhaps as a 'cluster' unit near the main Housing Association building which it is planned to construct. They hope that, in time to come, Alistair will be taken into the care of the Homes Foundation.

Fourth, they give some small cash legacies to friends, godchildren and a charity.

Fifth, they decide to participate in the Savings Plan, linked with life assurance, devised by Mencap. Under this plan they save money regularly, and the payments they make also buy them life insurance. In this way, if Mr Vernon dies before his retirement date in twenty years' time, the insurance money will be paid immediately, together with the savings he has made. If he survives to age 65, which he fully expects to do, a large sum of money, savings and life insurance, will be available for transfer to the City Foundation under the terms of his Will. Mr and Mrs Vernon write a detailed note explaining what the City Foundation needs to know about Alistair.

Mr and Mrs Rogers are less fortunate than the Vernons or the Westons. They do not own their home, and they have no cash assets to speak of. They have two children, the eldest of whom is mentally handicapped; both children are at school. They decide to start to make some savings out of their income, because Mrs Rogers is now able to go out to work, and they have extra help through the Attendance Allowance, which is payable for their eldest child. They join the Mencap Savings and Life Assurance Plan, just as Mr and Mrs Vernon did. Originally, they had assumed that, because they did not own their house, they could not take part in the Mencap Homes Foundation scheme, nor the Trustee Visitors Service. Talking to a member of Mencap's regional staff, they realise that a shortage of money is no bar to their child being accepted into a Homes Foundation home; in the home created by their own local Mencap Society, several people are already living whose parents died some time ago, and who certainly made no contribution at all.

If all goes well, Mr and Mrs Rogers will have saved some thousands of pounds by the time they retire. They make wills, leaving the money payable under the Savings and Life Assurance Plan to the City Foundation, with the written suggestion that, if enough cash is available, the Foundation might make a contribution to the Mencap Trustee Visitors Service. As an alternative, they could have nominated the City

Foundation to receive the money direct under the Life Assurance Policy, but they decided to make this donation by will, in case they might want to change their minds at a later date. Any other property they may have when they die, the Rogers leave to their non-handicapped child.

The above examples merely show some ways in which the parents of a mentally handicapped child can make provision for the future, through the schemes that Mencap has created. Every family is different, and each owns different property. No handicapped person is excluded from any scheme simply on the ground that his family have no money.

As we have seen, the schemes described in this and previous chapters could be adapted by other charitable organisations to benefit groups of people with different kinds of handicap. Couples can also set up their own charitable trusts, though they must select the trustees carefully, and should choose people who are likely to outlive them and possibly also their child. These charitable trusts, including those created by Mencap, offer great tax advantages. In the first place, the income on any money or other assets given to them does not suffer income tax. Income on property in a legally binding trust will normally suffer tax at the basic rate, and there may also be levied the investment income surcharge; but income on charitable funds does not have to bear any tax at all. Moreover, if the value of assets in the charity increases on a sale and a reinvestment, there is no capital gains tax to pay, which would certainly not be the case with an ordinary trust.

Best of all, transfers to a charity are free of capital transfer tax. Thus a whole family can benefit from the transfer to a charity. To give an example, if a husband and wife are able to leave a total of £120,000 on their deaths, and want to give it to their three children, one of whom is handicapped, they can donate a one-third share (£40,000) to a charity. The result will be that the remaining two-thirds of their assets (which go to the non-handicapped children) will only bear capital transfer tax at a rate appropriate to £80,000, not £120,000. In this way, the other two children actually benefit by reason of the fact that one third of their parents' property has been transferred to a charity, not to a trust. The capital transfer tax on their shares is less than it would otherwise have been.

It is most important to remember, in case an individual parent is considering the creation of a scheme of this kind, that the law relating to charities, and specifically to trusts, is complied with. If it should emerge that there is in fact some kind of secret trust in operation (which does not apply to the Mencap schemes) then the charity's status will be in considerable danger, the income will be taxable, and the regulations regarding Supplementary Benefits and Part III accommodation will apply. In the case of private charities, set up by only a few parents, from which their own children are clearly receiving – and intended to receive – the benefit, the danger of a challenge is far greater than exists for national charities which are demonstrably operating so as to help a very wide range of beneficiaries.

In spite of the many problems described earlier in this book, there are therefore still ways in which the property of the parents of handicapped children can be given, by will or during their lives, in such a way that it does not become subject to a charge by a Statutory Authority, nor reduce Benefits paid to a handicapped person. Great care must be taken to ensure that no trusts are created, but it is now possible to make provision in a manner that helps a charity. The charity, in its turn, is free to provide benefits for all handicapped people, including the relative of those persons who have made donations – provided there is no legally binding obligation on its part, nor any form of secret trust.

Summary

To summarise: the options now open to parents and relatives who are considering what provision to make during their lives, and by will, are these:

1   They can give their property to someone other than their handicapped child. Although in some ways attractive, this has several disadvantages.
2   They can make a donation to a scheme such as the Mencap Trustee Visitors Service, which provides a visitor for a mentally handicapped person after his or her parents have both died.
3   They can - and should - set up a small trust for the handicapped child, limited to £1,200 or £3,000, whichever is appropriate.
4   They can make a donation to the Mencap Homes Foundation, or to a charity operating a similar scheme.
5   They can donate money or other assets, including the proceeds of a life insurance policy, to the Mencap City Foundation, or to a charity operating a similar scheme.

Parents and relatives can select any one of these options, or any combination of them, in whatever way they may decide, and as advised by their own solicitor.

Appendix I

SPECIMEN CLAUSES FOR WILLS AND TRUSTS

Clause A: Clause enabling Executors or Trustees to make a donation to the Mencap Homes Foundation, if a suitable home becomes available after the Testator's death.

Clause B: Clause giving financial support to a handicapped person until such time as its existence would deprive him of Benefits or give rise to a Local Authority charge.

Clause C: Clause making a donation (with a Nomination) to the Mencap Trustee Visitors Service.

Clause D: Clause donating property to Mencap for the purpose of the Homes Foundation.

Clause E: Similar Clause, but giving surviving spouse the right to live in the property as long as he/she wishes.

Clause F: Similar Clause, for use by Tenants in Common of Freehold or Leasehold property.

Clause G: Clause giving a donation of different types of property to the Mencap City Foundation.

This Appendix contains some specimen Clauses which may, at the discretion of the parents of handicapped children, and of their legal advisers, be inserted in Wills or in Trust Documents, when there is an intention to give a benefit to a handicapped person, or to a charity. Readers would be most unwise, however, to write their own Wills or to incorporate the Clauses set out here. The Clauses are intended as draft provisions, to be considered by a solicitor when preparing a Will for a client. Consideration should be given to the Regulations affecting Supplementary Benefits and Local Authority Part III accommodation, explained in Chapter 6.

Bearing in mind the above caveat, the Clauses that follow have been prepared by the author (who is the Legal Adviser to Mencap) in response to requests from parents and from solicitors who, over a period of years, have sought help. Many Clauses appear here in a form which has resulted from suggestions and amendments by solicitors themselves. In each case, a Clause is introduced by a brief description of the problem that it is intended to solve.

CLAUSE A

The intention of this Clause is to give maximum flexibility and maximum discretion to Executors and Trustees who have the task of administering a Trust Fund for the benefit of a handicapped person. At the time when the Trust is created, it may appear that there is no obviously suitable home to which the handicapped person can go on the deaths of his parents; yet the time may come, possibly some years after their deaths, when such a home is set up, or when an opportunity arises for the handicapped beneficiary to move into a place which is well suited to his needs. By way of example, there may be no Mencap Homes Foundation home, or other charitable establishment, in the area where the beneficiary lives, but there may be plans to create one. In the years to come, it is possible that a home, maybe several homes, will exist, in which case the addition of funds from a Trust may enable the right accommodation to be created for the benefit of several handicapped people, including the child of the parent who created the Trust.

I HEREBY AUTHORISE my Trustees to apply all or any part of my Estate as they may in their absolute discretion think fit in or towards any Scheme or Plan which in my

Trustees' opinion may provide adequate security and protection for my Son/Daughter . . . . during his/her life. I specifically declare that my Trustees may in exercising these powers transfer to any other body, society or person any part or the whole of my Estate as may in their opinion be necessary or desirable for the fulfilment of any such Scheme or Plan

CLAUSE B

This Clause is intended to give financial support to a handicapped person until such time as its existence would deprive him of State Benefits. To give an example, a man may want to give his daughter an income while she continues to live with her mother, or with another member of the family. The existence of the Trust may deprive her of Supplementary Benefit (see Chapter 6), but she may still be able to claim the Non-Contributory Invalidity Pension. However, if the time comes when she has to go into Local Authority Part III accommodation, the Trust will immediately cease, and the property will be held by the Trustees for someone else. As a result, the handicapped person will be deprived of the Benefit, but this is not likely to harm her in any way, as the property would otherwise have been used to pay the Local Authority its fees for providing accommodation.

UPON TRUST as to both capital and income to apply the same in their absolute discretion for the benefit of my Son/Daughter . . . . until such time as the Trust Fund and the income thereon or any part thereof shall be deemed to form part of the assets or resources of my said Son/Daughter so as to require him/her to make a contribution to the cost of providing him/her with residential accommodation And Subject Thereto (a) To retain upon the same trusts such part of the Trust Fund as shall not cause the same to be deemed to form part of the assets or resources of my said Son/Daughter so as to require him/her to make a contribution to the cost of providing him/her with residential accommodation and (b) To hold the remainder of the Trust Fund UPON TRUST for...........

CLAUSE C

The Mencap Trustee Visitors Service has already been mentioned in this book (Chapter 4). Some parents and relatives make donations to the Trust Fund which operates the Service during their lives, or by way of a Life Insurance Policy, but many prefer to make their donation by Will. In this case, the amount of the donation will depend on the cost of sponsoring a handicapped person at the time the Service is to operate. The Clause therefore takes the following form:

> I/WE give to the Mencap Trustee Visitors Service of the Royal Society for Mentally Handicapped Children & Adults of 123 Golden Lane London EC1Y 0RT the sum of Two Thousand Five Hundred Pounds (£2,500) OR such sum as shall at the date of my (our) death(s) equal the amount that shall at that time be currently required by the Society from any person wishing to make a cash donation to join the Service, whichever sum shall be the higher.

At the same time that the above Clause is inserted in a Will, donors are asked to complete a form which they return to Mencap. This reads as follows:

> Please note that I/We.........................of..... ....have by a Will/ Wills dated the........day of...........19..bequeathed to the Mencap Trustee Visitors Service of the Royal Society for Mentally Handicapped Children & Adults of 123 Golden Lane London EC1Y 0RT the sum of Two Thousand Five Hundred Pounds (£2,500) OR such sum as shall at the date of my/our death(s) equal the amount that

shall at that time be currently required by the Society from any person wishing to make a cash donation to join the Service, whichever sum shall be the higher.

The Executors of my Will are.............................
....and they have been instructed to notify you in the event of my/our death

CLAUSES D, E AND F

These three Clauses have been designed in connection with the Mencap Homes Foundation, but they could of course be simply adapted so as to apply to any other Charity. The intention is that the donor's child should be considered as a resident of a home that the Homes Foundation has set up or is about to set up. It is stressed (as explained in Chapter 8) that the Charity cannot be put under any binding legal obligation to house a particular person, or indeed to house him or her in a particular house.

In the case of gifts to the Homes Foundation (which is an integral part of the Royal Society for Mentally Handicapped Children & Adults), it is vital that the donors should first have communicated with the Royal Society, and have given full details of their handicapped child, on forms provided for the purpose. Not only does the Society want to know as much as possible about the handicapped person, but it also needs to know about the number of people who have it in mind to donate homes, and the areas of the country in which they live. Advance planning, involving the co-operation of local Mencap Societies, is absolutely essential. If it does not take place, then there is a very real risk that the intended gift may not be used, thus frustrating the wishes of all concerned. Solicitors acting for the families of handicapped people are particularly asked to see that consultation takes place.

Clause D is simple; it gives a property to Mencap, and underlines the fact that no form of contract or bargain is being made:

I GIVE my Freehold/Leasehold property No........
....or such other
property as shall be my residence at the date of my death
to the Royal Society for Mentally Handicapped Children
and Adults of 123 Golden Lane, London EC1Y ORT and
without imposing any trust or legally binding obligation
I REQUEST that the said Society will bear in mind the
needs of my Son/Daughter.......................

As is well known, if an old or infirm person has to move into
Local Authority accommodation and owns a freehold or
leasehold property, the Local Authority may be able to make a
charge for accommodating him or her, and this may result in
the sale of the property. This can be particularly frustrating to
members of his or her family, most especially where there is a
handicapped child whose parents want to make a gift to the
Homes Foundation. There are Regulations which enable Local
Authorities to set aside transfers of property made by people
who are trying to avoid the effect of the above rules. These
Regulations also apply to Supplementary Benefits. Regulation
4 (1) of the Supplementary Benefits (Resources) Regulations
1981 (SI 1981: No 1527) reads:

Any resource of which a member of the assessment unit has
deprived himself for the purpose of securing Supplementary
Benefit, or increasing the amount of any such Benefit, may be
treated as if it were still possessed by him.

These Regulations do not of course affect property transfers
made by people unless they are in Local Authority accommodation, or receiving Supplementary Benefit. So if a spouse who is
the sole owner of a property states, in his Will, that his
surviving spouse may live there for as long as he or she wishes,
but that when he or she ceases to do so, the property passes to
the Homes Foundation, then the Regulations will not come into
effect. A legacy giving effect to this might read as follows:

Clause E

> I GIVE my Freehold/Leasehold property No. . . . .
> or such other property as shall be my residence at the date
> of my death to my Trustees UPON TRUST to sell the same
> with the consent of my Husband/Wife . . . . and to
> convert the same into money with power to postpone such
> sale and conversion and subject thereto to permit my said
> Husband/Wife to reside therein for as long as he/she
> wishes, he/she being responsible for repairing, maintain-
> ing and insuring the same during his/her occupation
> thereof, and after he/she ceases permanently to reside
> therein I GIVE the same to the Royal Society for Mentally
> Handicapped Children & Adults of 123 Golden Lane
> London EC1Y 0RT. Without imposing any trust or legally
> binding obligation I request that the said Society shall
> bear in mind the interests of my Son/Daughter . . . .

Clause E is designed for the person who is the sole owner of a
property. Greater complications ensue when a husband and
wife own a property jointly; there is a danger that the Local
Authority charge might be payable by the survivor, especially if
they were, during their lives, 'joint tenants' of the freehold or
leasehold. (The phrase 'joint tenants' is a legal technicality, and
does not necessarily imply the existence of a tenancy, or the
payment of a rent.) In such circumstances as these, there are
these alternatives facing the parents:

a   They may decide to make an immediate gift of their
property (known as an 'inter vivos' gift) to the Homes
Foundation, such gift to take effect only upon the
survivor of them ceasing to reside there. This would avoid
the Local Authority charge, but it might limit the
couple's freedom to dispose of their home, or to change it
for another.

b   They may 'sever' the joint tenancy (another technical
legal phrase), and make Wills bequeathing their own
half-share to the Homes Foundation, subject to the

proviso that their spouse could continue to live there. By this means, any Local Authority charge would only attach to half the property.

Clause F is designed to give effect to Option b:

> I GIVE my equal half share of the Freehold/Leasehold property No................or such other property as shall be my residence at the date of my death, which I declare that I own as a Tenant in Common with my Husband/Wife............., to my Trustees UPON TRUST to sell the same with the consent of my said Husband/Wife and to convert the same into money with power to postpone such sale and conversion and subject thereto to permit my said Husband/Wife to reside therein for as long as he/she wishes, he/she being responsible for repairing, maintaining and insuring the same during his/her occupation thereof, and after he/she ceases permanently to reside therein I GIVE my said share to the Royal Society for Mentally Handicapped Children & Adults of 123 Golden Lane London EC1Y 0RT. Without imposing any trust or legally binding obligation I request that the said Society shall bear in mind the needs of my Son/Daughter................

Solicitors preparing Wills for clients may also feel it appropriate to insert a clause enabling the trustees to buy a replacement home at the request of the surviving spouse, to be held on the same terms as those set out in Clauses E and F.

CLAUSE G
This Clause covers donations to the Mencap City Foundation, the purpose of which is explained in Chapter 9. If a donation is to be made to the Foundation, then the person making the Will should also leave a note which gives full details of his handicapped relative, and of his likely future needs.

I GIVE:

a   My Freehold/Leasehold property No................

or such other property as shall be my residence at the date of my death

b   The sum of £............

c   All the proceeds of the Insurance Policy on my life No..............with.........(name of Life Insurance Company)

d   The following chattels, namely:

(Details of specific property, such as a car, jewellery, pictures, etc.)

e   (Any other property to be donated)

to the Mencap City Foundation of 123 Golden Lane London EC1Y 0RT and without imposing any trust or legally binding obligation I REQUEST that the said Foundation will bear in mind the needs of my Son/ Daughter..............

Appendix II

NOTES ON STATUTES, REGULATIONS AND DECIDED CASES

This Appendix contains notes on the legal implications of some decided cases, which have a particular significance for handicapped people. There are also notes on the effect of Statutes, Regulations and other rules. These are set out here because they are referred to in the book, and also because it can be troublesome to find them in the volumes of a Law Library. These notes are of course in no way a substitute for legal advice, for they may be applied in different ways to different families. Anyone in doubt about his legal position, or that of his handicapped child, should consult a solicitor, whose task his clients will make easier if they can refer him direct to the Statutes and Regulations that concern them, and to the relevant decided cases. This will save his time, and their money.

The contents of this Appendix are as follows:

Notes on Family Inheritance and Provision
Notes on Guardianship
Charities and the Bargain/Bounty rule
Notes on the Priority Rights of Handicapped people who are Homeless
Notes on Resources of people receiving Supplementary Benefit
Notes on Residential Care Homes
Notes on the Education Acts

NOTES ON FAMILY INHERITANCE AND PROVISION
Under the Inheritance (Provision for Family and Dependants)
Act 1975, it is possible to apply to a Court for the variation of
the terms of a Will, if the Testator has failed to make
reasonable provision for a dependant relative. What is 'reasonable' depends on the circumstances of the Testator, the size of
his estate, the degree of dependence of the relative and the
extent of his own resources, and any other factors that a Court
decides should be taken into consideration.

On page 119 of this book there is some discussion of the
possibility that claims may be made to vary the provisions of
Wills in which little or no provision has been made for a
dependant handicapped child. Reference is made to the case of
Re E (deceased), E v E (1966 2 All E.R. at P. 44).

In Re E, there was a dispute over a relatively small estate. A
testator left all his property to the woman with whom he had
been living, and his wife sought to have reasonable provision
made for herself. The claim failed, but the Judge made some
remarks on the relevance of the availability of State Benefits.
He accepted the submission of the defendant's counsel that, as
the estate of the deceased was small and the only effect of
making provision for the plaintiff was to relieve the National
Assistance Fund (as it then was named), it was not unreasonable for the testator to take the view that there was no point in
his making provision for the plaintiff.

However, the Judge went on to say that the fact that those
who are badly off can obtain National Assistance (now
Supplementary Benefit), and are not left to starve, would
not in his judgement afford any good reason, of itself, to justify
a deceased making no provision for a claimant out of a very
large estate. The purpose of the legislation was not to require a
deceased to keep his dependants above the breadline, but to
ensure that reasonable provision was made for them, having
regard to all the circumstances. It would be no answer to a
claim by a poor widow against her rich husband's estate that

she can always have resort to State Benefits, and that he need therefore not make provision for her.

The Judge went on to draw attention to the fact that there is authority (*Re Inns, Inns v Wallace* (1947) 2 All E.R. 308) for the proposition that jurisdiction under the Family Provision (Inheritance) legislation should be cautiously, if not sparingly, exercised, even where the estate is one of magnitude. It is for this reason that the view is put, on page 120 of this book, that if a deceased makes provision for his handicapped relative up to the maximum amount that will not deprive him of Supplementary Benefits, or the maximum figure that will not require him to pay for Local Authority Part III accommmodation, it is most unlikely that a judge would agree to vary the terms of the Will. Of course, if an estate is so large that the income on the share bequeathed to, or in trust for, a handicapped person is so great that there could still be a benefit in real terms for the handicapped relative in spite of the loss of Benefits and the levy of the Local Authority's charge, then an application to vary the terms of the Will would be more likely to succeed. To determine whether this might be the case, a Testator would have to make complex calculations involving the annual cost (say) of maintaining a person in a Local Authority home, the probable income (after deduction of tax) that would be available to meet such cost, and the size of the fund that would have to be set aside to provide that income.

NOTES ON GUARDIANSHIP

The Mental Health Act 1983
With effect from the 30th September, 1983, this Act made considerable changes in the law relating to people who are mentally ill, and to those who are mentally handicapped. It must of course be understood that these are two entirely different conditions.

Section 7 of the Act reads as follows:

Guardianship

Section 7 (1)   A patient who has attained the age of 16 years may be received into guardianship, for the period allowed by the following provisions of this Act, in pursuance of an application (in this Act referred to as 'a guardianship application') made in accordance with this section.

(2)   A guardianship application may be made in respect of a patient on the grounds that:

(a)   he is suffering from mental disorder, being mental illness, severe mental impairment, psychopathic disorder or mental impairment and his mental disorder is of a nature or degree which warrants his reception into guardianship under this section; and

(b)   it is necessary in the interests of the welfare of the patient or for the protection of other persons that the patient should be so received.

(3)   A guardianship application shall be founded on the written recommendations in the prescribed form of two registered medical practitioners, including in each case a statement that in the opinion of the practitioner the conditions set out in subsection (2) above are complied with; and each such recommendation shall include:

(a)   such particulars as may be prescribed of the grounds for that opinion so far as it relates to the conditions set out in paragraph (a) of that subsection; and

(b)   a statement of the reasons for that opinion so far as it relates to the conditions set out in paragraph (b) of that subsection.

(4)   A guardianship application shall state the age of the patient or, if his exact age is not known to the applicant, shall state (if it be the fact) that the patient is believed to have attained the age of 16 years.

(5) The person named as guardian in a guardianship application may be either a local social services authority or any other person (including the applicant himself); but a guardianship application in which a person other than a local social services authority is named as guardian shall be of no effect unless it is accepted on behalf of that person by the local social services authority for the area in which he resides and shall be accompanied by a statement in writing by that person that he is willing to act as guardian.

Section 1 (2) of the Act contains definitions of the phrases 'mental disorder', 'severe mental impairment', 'mental impairment' and 'psychopathic disorder', mentioned in Section 7 (2) (a) above. It reads as follows:

Section 1 (2) In this Act:
'mental disorder' means mental illness, arrested or incomplete development of mind, psychopathic disorder and any other disorder or disability of mind and 'mentally disordered' shall be construed accordingly;
'severe mental impairment' means a state of arrested or incomplete development of mind which includes severe impairment of intelligence and social functioning and is associated with abnormally aggressive or seriously irresponsible conduct on the part of the person concerned and 'severely mentally impaired' shall be construed accordingly;
'mental impairment' means a state of arrested or incomplete development of mind (not amounting to severe mental impairment) which includes significant impairment of intelligence and social functioning and is associated with abnormally aggressive or seriously irresponsible conduct on the part of the person concerned and 'mentally impaired' shall be construed accordingly;
'psychopathic disorder' means a persistent disorder or disability of mind (whether or not including significant impairment of intelligence) which results in abnormally

aggressive or seriously irresponsible conduct on the part of the person concerned.

The great majority of mentally handicapped people do not come within the provisions of the Act. They are normally not mentally ill, and the words 'abnormally aggressive or seriously irresponsible conduct' can only refer to very few of them. It has been estimated that there are in fact only some hundreds of mentally handicapped people who come into these categories; a very high proportion of them are in hospital, or some other form of institutional care.

CHARITIES AND THE BARGAIN/BOUNTY RULE

A major reason for the creation of the Mencap Homes Foundation was that parents wished to give their homes to the Royal Society for Mentally Handicapped Children and Adults, and thus assure for their child a permanent home, through a legally binding arrangement with the Society. This posed a considerable problem because of the decision by Rowlatt, J. in *C.I.R. v Society for the Relief of Widows and Orphans of Medical Men* (1926) 11 T.C.I at p. 22. The judge said:

> It seems to me that when it is said that the relief of poverty is a charity within the meaning of the rule which we are discussing, that does mean the relief of poverty, by way of bounty; it does not mean the relief of poverty by way of bargain.

The result is that, if a charitable organisation receives gifts which are conditional on a child being accommodated for life, it stands in danger of losing its charitable status, because it is entering into a bargain. For this reason, the charity cannot legally bind itself to provide a service for a particular person in return for a gift of money or other property. It is, however, entitled to consider the needs of a person related to and/or nominated by the donor. A charity that meets such needs, but that also devotes the property thus received to other persons within the ambit of its work, is not likely to find itself in danger of losing its status.

NOTES ON THE PRIORITY RIGHTS OF HANDICAPPED PEOPLE WHO ARE HOMELESS

Under the terms of the National Assistance Act 1948, Local Authorities are under a duty to provide homes for people who cannot find a home of their own. There are considerable variations between different Local Authorities in the way in which this duty is carried out, and in 1977 the Housing (Homeless Persons) Act was passed, making it clear that there are some categories of people who have a priority right to be found accommodation. The Act is long and its provisions complex; legal advice should certainly be obtained by anyone who wishes to see that the rights of a handicapped person are enforced. However, the most significant parts of the Act are set out below:

Housing (Homeless Persons) Act 1977

Section 2   (1)   For the purposes of this Act a homeless person threatened with homelessness has a priority need for accommodation when the housing authority are satisfied that he is within one of the following categories:

    (c)   he or any person who resides or might reasonably be expected to reside with him is vulnerable as a result of old age, mental illness or handicap or physical disability or other special reason.

Section 4   (5)   Where:

    (a)   they (*the Local Authority*) are satisfied

      (i)   that he is homeless, and

      (ii)   that he has a priority need, but

    (b)   they are not satisfied that he became homeless intentionally, their duty, subject to Section 5 below, is to secure that accommodation becomes available for his occupation.

Section 5   (1)   A housing authority are not subject to a duty under Section 4 (5) above:

(a)   if they are of the opinion:
   (i)   that neither the person who applied to them for accommodation or for assistance in obtaining accommodation nor any person who might reasonably be expected to reside with him has a local connection with their area, and
   (ii) that the person who so applied or a person who might reasonably be expected to reside with him has a local connection with another housing authority's area.

This Act also has provisions under which financial and other help may be given to voluntary organisations who are concerned with homelessness.

NOTES ON RESOURCES OF PEOPLE RECEIVING SUPPLEMENTARY BENEFITS

On page 111, there is an explanation of the effect of the Regulations concerning the resources of handicapped people. There follows an extract from Statutory Instrument No 1527 of 1981, entitled: 'SOCIAL SECURITY. The Supplementary Benefit (Resources) Regulations 1981' (as amended):

Part II. Capital Resources

Calculation of capital resources

5   Except in so far as regulation 6 provides that certain resources shall be disregarded, the amount of a claimant's capital resources to be taken into account shall be the whole of his capital resources assessed where applicable:
   (a)   at their current market or surrender value less:
      (i)   in the case of land, 10 per cent., and in any other case, any sum which would be attributable to expenses of sale, and
      (ii) any outstanding debt or mortgage secured on them;
   (b)   in the case of a National Savings Certificate:
      (i)   if purchased from an issue the sale of which ceased before the 1st July preceding the date of

assessment, at the value which it would have had on that 1st July had it been purchased on the last day of that issue.

(ii)   in any other case at its purchase price.

Capital resources to be disregarded

6   (1)   In calculating a claimant's capital resources the following shall be disregarded:

(a)   the value of:

   (i)   the home,

  (ii)   any premises which have been acquired and not yet occupied by the assessment unit but which it is intended will be the home within 6 months of the date of acquisition or such longer period as is reasonable in the circumstances,

 (iii)   any premises which are for sale and the value of which it would be reasonable in all the circumstances to disregard for such period as the benefit officer may estimate as that during which the sale will be completed,

 (iv)   any premises of which the whole or part is occupied by an aged or incapacitated relative of any member of the assessment unit,

  (v)   the assets of any business which is owned, in whole or in part, by a member of the assessment unit, for such period as in the opinion of the benefit them,

 (vi)   any reversionary interest,

except in relation to any part of premises which, having regard to all the circumstances, it would be practicable or reasonable to regard as a property which could be realised separately;

(b)   any sum attributable to the proceeds of sale of a home which is to be used for the purchase of another home within 6 months of the date of sale or such longer period as is reasonable in the circumstances;

    (c) the value of any personal possessions except any which:
- (i) are in the nature of an investment,
- (ii) have been acquired by converting, for the purpose of acquiring a right to or increasing the amount of supplementary benefit, capital resources which would not have fallen to be disregarded under this paragraph, or
- (iii) having regard to their nature, use, likely value and the standard of living of other persons in similar circumstances, it would be unreasonable to disregard;

    (d) any savings of mobility allowance paid under the Social Security Act which the recipient intends to use in connexion with mobility;

    (e) for a period not exceeding 12 months from the date of receipt, any arrears of:
- (i) attendance or mobility allowance paid under the Social Security Act,
- (ii) supplementary benefit;

    (f) any sum which is deposited with a housing association as defined in section 189(1) of the Housing Act 1957(a) or section 208(1) of the Housing (Scotland) Act 1966(b) as a condition of occupying the home.

(2) Where the value of a claimant's capital resources (including those of a partner or dependant) as calculated in accordance with these regulations is £3,000 or less, those resources shall, except in so far as any provision of the Act or regulations made pursuant to it provides otherwise, be disregarded.

Maximum capital resources for entitlement to pension or allowance
7 Subject to regulation 8, where the value of a claimant's capital resources (including those of a partner or dependant)

as calculated in accordance with these regulations exceeds £3,000, the claimant shall not be entitled to pension or allowance.

Effect of capital resources of dependants

8   (1)   Where a claimant's capital resources as calculated in accordance with these regulations:

(a)   exceed the sum specified in regulation 7; but

(b)   would be reduced to or below that sum if the capital resources of a dependant were disregarded,

the capital resources of that dependant shall be disregarded as a capital resource, but shall be treated as producing a weekly income resource equal to the weekly requirements which would be applicable to that dependant under Parts II and III of the Requirements Regulations (normal and additional requirements).

(2)   Where a claimant has more than one dependant who has capital resources, paragraph (1) shall apply only to that dependant or those dependants to whom the application of that paragraph in the determination of the claimant's title to pension or allowance would produce the result most favourable to the claimant.

Tribunal Decision No. R (SB) 25/83

The following is a summary of this decision, which merits detailed study.

A claimant, who was in receipt of supplementary allowance, was one of three daughters and became a beneficiary under her late mother's will. The assets consisted of the freehold property in which the claimant lived, and investments valued at some £4,700. The will provided, *inter alia*, that no sale should be made of the house in which the claimant lived during her lifetime without her consent. The trustee was directed to invest the residue and pay the income from it to the claimant; after her death to hold upon the same trusts in equal shares for such of the children of the claimant's sisters as should be living at the claimant's death. The supplementary benefit officer decided that the claimant was not entitled to supplementary allowance on the grounds that, being the only beneficiary, her capital resources calculated in accordance with Regulation 4 (8) of the Supplementary Benefit (Resources) Regulations 1981 exceeded £2,000 (the claimant being notionally entitled to the capital resources valued at £4,700). On appeal, the Tribunal considered that, having regard to the terms of the trust and the duty of the trustee to balance the interests of the tenant for life and the remaindermen, the claimant should not be treated as possessing any part of the trust fund under Regulation 4 (8)(b) of the Resources Regulations. The supplementary benefit officer appealed to a Social Security Commissioner.

The appeal was *allowed*. The Social Security Commissioner said that 'beneficiaries' under a trust include all persons who may receive benefits from the resources in question under any trust or power in the trust instruments. In deciding the appropriate share, the purpose as well as the terms of the trust, whether express or implied, should be considered; there are cases where a claimant may properly be treated as entitled to the whole of the resources held under a trust, even though that trust has other beneficiaries.

A statement by a trustee that it is not intended to exercise a discretion to pay capital (or income) in favour of a claimant if that would reduce the amount of supplementary benefit payable to the claimant is, however, not material.

The fixing of the appropriate share is not intended to be made on the basis of the actuarial or market value of the 'interests'. The method to be adopted is after consideration of the number of the beneficiaries, the terms express or implied of the trust and the other circumstances, having regard to the real probabilities under the trust.

Comment: The true intent of parents *is* in fact to benefit their handicapped child when they create a trust. This intent will become apparent as the trust is administered. It is for these reasons that it is considered that the Mencap Homes Foundation and the Mencap City Foundation are more satisfactory, as they exist for handicapped people generally. Their assets are held by a charity, and are not subject to a trust.

NOTES ON RESIDENTIAL CARE HOMES

Under the Health and Social Services and Social Security Adjudications Act 1983, there are provisions relating to Charges for Local Authority Services, for the Registration of Residential Care Homes, and for the Conduct of Homes. Some excerpts from the Act are set out below:

Part VII - Charges for Local Authority Services

17 (1) Subject to subsection (3) below, an authority providing a service to which this section applies may recover such charge (if any) for it as they consider reasonable.

(2) This section applies to services provided under the following enactments:

> (a) Section 29 of the National Assistance Act 1948 (welfare arrangements for blind, deaf, dumb and crippled persons, etc.).

(3) If a person:

> (a) avails himself of a service to which this section applies, and
>
> (b) satisfies the authority supplying the service that his means are insufficient for it to be reasonably practicable for him to pay for the service the amount which he would otherwise be obliged to pay for it,

the authority shall not require him to pay more for it than it appears to them that it is reasonably practicable for him to pay.

Schedule 4 - Registered Homes

Part I - Residential Care Homes - Requirement of Registration

1 (1) Subject to the following provisions of this para-

graph, registration under this Part of this Schedule is required in respect of any establishment which provides or is intended to provide, whether for reward or not, residential accommodation with both board and personal care for persons in need of personal care by reason of old age, disablement, past or present dependence on alcohol or drugs or past or present mental disorder.

(4)   Registration under this Part of this Schedule is not required in respect of an establishment which provides or is intended to provide residential accommodation with both board and personal care for fewer than four persons, excluding persons carrying on or intending to carry on the home or employed or intended to be employed there and their relatives.

19   (1)   The Secretary of State may make regulations as to the conduct of residential homes, and in particular:

(a)   as to the facilities and services to be provided in such homes;

(b)   as to the numbers and qualifications of staff to be employed in such homes;

(c)   as to the numbers of suitably qualified and competent staff to be on duty in such homes;

(d)   as to the records to be kept and notices to be given in respect of persons received into such homes;

(e)   as to the notification of events occurring in such homes:

(f)   as to the giving of notice by a person of a description specified in the regulations of periods during which any person of a description so specified proposes to be absent from a home;

(g)   as to the information to be supplied in such a notice;

(h)   making provision for children under the age of 18 years who are resident in such homes to receive a religious upbringing appropriate to the religious persuasion to which they belong;

(i)   as to the form of registers to be kept by registration authorities for the purposes of this Part of this Schedule and the particulars to be contained in them; and
(j)   as to the information to be supplied on application for registration.

There are also provisions for the inspection of homes, and for prosecutions that may follow a breach of the regulations.

NOTES ON THE EDUCATION ACTS

Education Act 1944 (as amended)
The Local Education Authority must secure provision of education for pupils up to the age of 19, including mentally handicapped people.

Education (Handicapped Children) Act 1970
Severely mentally handicapped children can no longer be classified as unsuitable for education at school.

Education Act 1980
A Special School maintained by a Local Education Authority must include at least two parent governors. Parents have the right to information on schools.

Education Act 1981
Parents have the right to ask for an assessment of their child's needs, and to be provided with a copy of the statement made by the Authority indicating the provision they intend to make.

Appendix III

RECOMMENDED PUBLICATIONS

There are many useful publications for the parents and relatives of handicapped people. The following are particularly recommended:

TITLES IN THE SOUVENIR PRESS HUMAN HORIZONS SERIES

Disability, Theatre and Education by Richard Tomlinson, 1982.
Dramatising experiences and feelings through the theatre.
Down's Syndrome by Cliff Cunningham, 1982.
A guide for parents.
Drama for Mentally Handicapped Children by Ann B. McClintock, 1984.
Drama therapy as an aid to education and development of skills.
Gardening is for Everyone by Audrey Cloet and Chris Underhill, 1982.
A week-by-week guide for people with handicaps.
Helping Your Handicapped Baby by Cliff Cunningham and Patricia Sloper, 1978.
A Home of Their Own by Victoria Shennan, 1983.
A survey of current schemes to place mentally handicapped people in independent homes in the community.
Learning to Cope by Edward Whelan and Barbara Speake, 1979
Helping mentally handicapped adolescents to become more independent. Gives a chart for assessing individual needs and abilities.

Let's Join In by Dorothy M. Jeffree and Sally Cheseldine, 1984.

Preparing young mentally handicapped people for joining in the leisure pursuits of their non-handicapped peers.

Music for Mentally Handicapped People by Miriam Wood, 1983.

Out of Doors with Handicapped People by Mike Cotton, 1981.

The pleasures of outdoor activities.

Outdoor Adventure for Handicapped People by Mike Cotton, 1983.

More ambitious pursuits, ranging from rock climbing and caving to sailing and fishing.

Starting Off by Chris Kiernan, Rita Jordan and Chris Saunders, 1978.

Techniques for developing social and communication skills.

Teaching the Handicapped Child by Dorothy M. Jeffree, Roy McConkey and Simon Hewson, 1977.

Assessment and teaching schemes.

We Can Speak for Ourselves by Paul Williams and Bonnie Shoultz, 1982.

Self-advocacy by mentally handicapped people.

The Wheelchair Child by Philippa Russell, 2nd edition 1984.

PUBLICATIONS OF THE ROYAL SOCIETY FOR
MENTALLY HANDICAPPED CHILDREN AND ADULTS
(MENCAP)

Tongue-Tied by Joey Deacon, 1982.

The story of a man with cerebral palsy, written by himself.

Drama Games by Bernie Warren, 1981.

Games for mentally handicapped people.

Stress in Families with a Handicapped Child by Margaret Crozier, 1982.

After Sixteen by Ann Henshaw, 1979.
Towards a Full Life by Eileen Baranyay, 1981.
Residential Care for Mentally Handicapped People by Wynne Jones, 1982.
Pengwern Hall by Martin Weinberg, 1982.
   Training towards independence for mentally handicapped people.
'Stamina' Papers
   Checklists of minimum standards for provision of services for mentally handicapped people:
   1   Education in Schools
   2   Services for mentally handicapped people over 16
   3   Residential care for mentally handicapped people
   4   Hospitals for mentally handicapped people

OTHER PUBLICATIONS
   Autistic Children: a Guide for Parents by Dr Lorna Wing, Constable, 2nd edition, 1980.
   The Educational and Social Needs of Children with Severe Handicap by Mildred Stevens, Edward Arnold, 2nd edition, 1976.
   Give Us the Chance by Kay Latto, The Disabled Living Foundation, 1981.
   Sport and physical recreation with mentally handicapped people.
   Handicapped in a Social World by Ann Brechin, Penny Liddiard and John Swain, Hodder & Stoughton in association with the Open University Press, 1981.
   The disabled relationship, styles of living, professional support and integrated living.
   The Handicapped Person in the Community by David Boswell and Janet Eingrove, The Open University Press.
   Learning to Live with MS by Robin Dowie, Robert Povey and Gillian Whitley, Multiple Sclerosis Society of Great Britain and Northern Ireland, 1981.
   Mental Handicap: Services for the Mentally Handicapped in

Britain by Nigel Malin, David Race and Glenys Jones, Croom Helm, 1980.

Mentally Handicapped People: Living and Learning by David Clarke, Bailliére Tindall, 1982.
Brings together examples of research and practice.

Music for the Handicapped Child by J. Alvin, Oxford University Press, 1976.

The Nature of Special Education: People, Places and Change by Tony Booth and June Statham, Croom Helm in association with the Open University Press, 1982.

People Not Patients: Problems and Policies in Mental Handicap by Peter Mittler (ed.), Methuen, 1979.

Physical Education for Special Needs by Lilian Groves (ed.), Cambridge University Press, 1979.

Remedial Drama: A Handbook for Teachers and Therapists by Sue Jennings, Pitman, 1978.

Sex and the Handicapped Child by Dr Wendy Greengross, National Marriage Guidance Council, 1980.
The emotional and sexual needs of handicapped people.

Sex and the Mentally Handicapped Child by Michael and Ann Craft, Routledge & Kegan Paul, 2nd edition 1982.

Appendix IV

NAMES AND ADDRESSES OF VOLUNTARY ORGANISATIONS

This Appendix consists of a list of the names and addresses of voluntary organisations, from which parents and other family members may be able to get help and advice. Often, the organisations named will have a Legal or Welfare & Rights Department, or will be able to refer enquirers to a solicitor who can help them. They will also know the names of other professionals whose work is mentioned in Chapter 5. When a parent is in doubt whether the advice he has received is correct, or does not know whom to consult, the relevant organisation will often be able to help.

MENTAL HANDICAP
The Royal Society for Mentally Handicapped Children and Adults - known as MENCAP - of 123 Golden Lane, London, EC1Y 0RT (Tel: 01-253-9433), can advise on housing, educational, legal and social matters. It has an excellent bookshop (from which the publications mentioned in Appendix III can be obtained). It runs the entire nationwide network of Gateway Clubs, operates the Pathway Employment Scheme in various parts of the country, and generally represents mentally handicapped people and their families. The Society has training establishments, where handicapped people spend up to two years in training for work, or being equipped with much-needed social skills. Normally, enquiries about Mencap's work should be made to one of the twelve Regional Offices of the Society:

Eastern Counties Region
63a Churchgate Street, Bury St. Edmunds, Suffolk IP33 1RL.
(Tel: 0284-3526)

East Midlands Region
79/81 Mount Street, Nottingham NG1 6HE.
(Tel: 0602-410877)

Home Counties North Region
5 College Street, St. Albans, Herts AL3 4PW.
(Tel: 56-52245)

Metropolitan Region
115 Golden Lane, London EC1Y 0TJ. (Tel: 01-250-4105)

Northern Region
169 Durham Road, Gateshead, Tyne & Wear.
(Tel: 0632-775818)

North-West Region
Brentwood, Long Street, Middleton, Manchester M24 3DW.
(Tel: 061-654-8000)

South-East Region
Adjacent to Colebrook Day Centre, Greensand Road, Redhill,
Surrey RH1 1PT. (Tel: 91-67531)

Mencap in Wales
169a City Road, Cardiff CF2 3JB. (Tel: 0222-494933)

South-West Region
17 High Street, Taunton, Somerset TA1 3PJ.
(Tel: 0823-88061)

West Midlands Region
84 Aldridge Road, Perry Barr, Birmingham B42 2TP.
(Tel: 021-356-7306)

Yorkshire & Humberside Region
43 East Parade, Harrogate, North Yorkshire.
(Tel: 0423-68162)

Northern Ireland Region
4 Annadale Avenue, Belfast BT7 3JH. (Tel: 0232-691351)

There is a separate organisation in Scotland, the Scottish Society for the Mentally Handicapped, of 13 Elm Bank Street, Glasgow G2 4QA (Tel: 041-556-3882). It is not connected with the Royal Society for Mentally Handicapped Children and Adults, but of course maintains friendly relations with that organisation.

Other organisations connected with mental handicap are:

Down's Children's Association
Quinborne Community Centre, Ridgeacre Road, Birmingham B32 2TW.

British Institute for Mental Handicap
Information and Resource Centre, Wolverhampton Road, Kidderminster, Worcestershire DY10 3PP. (Tel: 0562-850251)

Association of Parents of Vaccine-damaged Children
Mrs Rosemary Fox, 2 Church Street, Shipston-on-Stour, Warwickshire CV36 4AP. (Tel: 0608-61595)

One-to-One (Contacts for mentally handicapped people in hospital)
123-25 Gloucester Place, London W1H 3PJ.
(Tel: 01-486-0074)

Jewish Society for the Mentally Handicapped
Stanmore Cottage, Old Church Lane, Stanmore, Middlesex.
(Tel: 01-954-0257)

Sports Association for People with Mental Handicaps
The Sports Council, 16 Upper Woburn Place, London WC1H
0QP. (Tel: 01-388-1277)

PHYSICAL HANDICAP
Help and advice may be obtained from the following:

Aidis Trust (Electronic aids for severely disabled people)
Willowbrook, Mursley, Milton Keynes, Bucks MK17
0JA.

Autistic Children, National Society for
276 Willesden Lane, London NW2 5RB. (Tel: 01-451-3844)

Blind, British Talking Book Service for the
Nuffield Library, Mount Pleasant, Wembley, Middlesex.

Blind, Royal National Institute for the
224 Great Portland Street, London W1N 6AV.
(Tel: 01-388-1266)

Telephone for the Blind Fund
Mynthurst, Leigh, Near Reigate, Surrey. (Tel: 0293-862546)

COPE (Family Groups)
19/29 Woburn Place, London WC1H 0LY.
(Tel: 01-278-7048)

British Deaf Association
38 Victoria Place, Carlisle CA1 1HU. (Tel: 0228-20188)

National Deaf Children's Society
45 Hereford Road, London W2 5AH. (Tel: 01-229-9272)

Deaf, Royal National Institute for the
105 Gower Street, London WC1E 6AH. (Tel: 01-387-8033)

Link Centre for Deafened People (Residential help)
19 Hartfield Road, Eastbourne, East Sussex BN21 2AR.
(Tel: 0323-638230)

Deaf Blind and Rubella Handicapped, National Association for
311 Grays Inn Road, London WC1X 8PT. (Tel: 01-278-1000)

Deaf and Dumb, Royal Association in Aid of the
27 Old Oak Road, Acton, London W3 7HN.
(Tel: 01-743-6187)

Disabled Living Foundation
346 Kensington High Street, London W14 8NS.
(Tel: 01-602-2491).

Disablement Income Group
Attlee House, Toynbee Hall, 28 Commercial Street, London E1
6LR. (Tel: 01-247-2128)

Disability Alliance (Publishers of *Disability Rights Handbook*)
25 Denmark Street, London WC1 8NJ. (Tel: 01-240-0806)

Disability and Rehabilitation, Royal Association for (RADAR)
25 Mortimer Street, London W1N 8AB. (Tel: 01-637-5400)

Centre for the Environment for the Handicapped
126 Albert Street, London NW1 7NF. (Tel: 01-482-2247)

Family Fund
PO Box 50, York YO1 1UY. (Tel: 0904-21115)

Friedrich's Ataxia Group
12c Worplesdon Road, Guildford, Surrey GU2 6RW.
(Tel: 0483-503133)

Handicapped Adventure Playgrounds Association
Fulham Palace, Bishops Avenue, London SW6 6EA.
(Tel: 01-736-4443)

Handicapped Children, Voluntary Council for
National Children's Bureau, 8 Wakley Street, London EC1V
7QE. (Tel: 01-278-9441)

Hard of Hearing, British Association for
6 Great James Street, London WC1N 3DA.

National Association of Leagues of Hospital Friends
565 Fulham Road, London SW6 1ES. (Tel: 01-730-0103)

Hyper-Active Children's Support Group
59 Meadowside, Angmering, West Sussex.
(Tel: 0243-551313)

Mental Health, National Association for (MIND)
22 Harley Street, London W1N 2ED. (Tel: 01-637-0741)

In Touch Trust (Children with some degree of retardation)
10 Norman Road, Sale, Cheshire M33 3DF.
(Tel: 061-962-4441)

Motability
91-93 Charterhouse Street, London EC1M 6BT.
(Tel: 01-253-1211)

Multiple Sclerosis Society
286 Munster Road, Fulham, London SW6 6AP.
(Tel: 01-381-4022)

Muscular Dystrophy Group of Great Britain
Natrass House, 35 Macaulay Road, London SW4 0QP.
(Tel: 01-720-8055)

Network for the Handicapped
35 Emerald Street, London WC1. (Tel: 01-504-3001)

Partially Sighted Society
40 Wordsworth Street, Hove, East Sussex BN3 5BH.
(Tel: 0273-736053)

SESAME (Movement and drama for mentally and physically disabled)
27 Blackfriars Road, London SE1. (Tel: 01-633-9705)

Sexual Problems of the Disabled (SPOD)
14 Peto Place, London NW1 4PT. (Tel: 01-486-9823)

SHAPE (Creative activities for the handicapped)
9 Fitzroy Square, London W1P 6AE. (Tel: 01-388-9622)

The Spastics Society
12 Park Crescent, London W1N 4EQ. (Tel: 01-636-5020)

Swimming Clubs for the Handicapped, National Association of
219 Preston Drive, Brighton, Sussex BN1 6FL.
(Tel: 0273-559470)

Talking Books for the Handicapped
National Listening Library, 12 Lant Street, London SE1 1QR.
(Tel: 01-407-9417)

PLAY MATTERS Toy Libraries Association
Seabrook House, Wyllyotts Manor, Darkes Lane, Potters Bar,
Herts. (Tel: 77-44571)

Toyaids Trust (Toys for Handicapped Children)
Lodbourne Green, Gillingham, Dorset. (Tel: 07476-2256)

Leaflets from the Department of Health & Social Security
The DHSS Leaflets Unit is at PO Box 21, Stanmore, Middlesex
HA7 1AY. If you are unable to obtain the leaflets you need from
the local DHSS office, the Leaflets Unit can supply them.

Tables of Cases and Statutes

Index